TABLE OF CONTENTS

MUSCULAR FITNESS THROUGH RESISTANCE TRAINING

Second Edition

by

Tom R. Thomas, Ph.D.
Professor, Exercise Physiology
University of Missouri
Columbia, Missouri

eddie bowers publishing, inc.
2600 Jackson Street
Dubuque, Iowa 52001

ACKNOWLEDGEMENTS

I am very grateful to a variety of individuals who helped me on this book. I especially thank Dr. Carole Zebas and Nancy King for writing chapters. The review and comments of Dr. John A. Roberts also are appreciated. Kris Williams and John Araujo served as models for the photographs, and I am grateful for their talent and patience. I appreciate the assistance of Dr. Carole Zebas who shot some of the photographs and Steve Hill who helped during the photography sessions. Thanks to my wife, Susan, for editorial assistance. I am grateful to the friendly people at the fitness equipment companies for providing photographs; a special note of appreciation is extended to those at Universal, Soloflex, and Hydra-Fitness for providing the cover photos. I also thank my many mentors, colleagues, and students who have shared their knowledge and expertise with me.

eddie bowers publishing, inc.
2600 Jackson Street
Dubuque, Iowa 52001

ISBN 0-945483-09-0

Copyright © 1986, First Edition
           1991, Second Edition
          by *eddie bowers publishing, inc.*

Printed in the United States of America.

9 8 7 6 5 4 3 2 1

ABBREVIATIONS USED IN THIS BOOK

Term	Abbreviation
adenosine triphosphate	ATP
beats per minute	bpm
calcium	Ca^{++}
carbohydrate	CHO
cardiovascular	CV
creatine phosphate	CP
circuit resistance training	CRT
essential amino acids	EAA
fast-twitch	FT
gram	g
heartbeats per minute	bpm
high density lipoprotein cholesterol	HDL-C
kilocalories (also Calories)	kcal (also Cal)
kilogram	kg
low density lipoprotein cholesterol	LDL-C
magnesium	Mg^+
one repetition maximum	1 RM
polyunsaturated fat	PUFA
pound	lb
recommended dietary allowance	RDA
saturated fat	SFA
slow-twitch	ST
triglyceride	TG
unsaturated fat	UFA

INTRODUCTION:

WHY RESISTANCE TRAINING?

Total physical fitness encompasses a variety of definitions and interpretations. Virtually every magazine and newspaper and every celebrity has a new "can't miss" method of getting into shape. Many different body functions are targets of the various fitness programs. Often specific kinds of exercise are necessary to optimally affect a given body system. But in many cases, the fitness of different systems is intertwined, and most exercise programs affect many physiological functions.

Many aspects of health are benefitted by physical fitness. These include cardiovascular efficiency, muscular strength and tone, body weight and percent body fat, joint and muscular flexibility, gastrointestinal function, and psychological well-being. Each of these aspects is important to overall health and the prevention of disease. Statistics collected over the world illustrate that active populations are healthier than sedentary groups. Virtually any type of activity can be beneficial, but what are the best types of exercise? Usually an exercise regimen emphasizes one fitness element over the others. In endurance training, the cardiovascular system is emphasized with little time allotted to other types of workouts. In resistance training, muscular strength is emphasized with cardiovascular fitness sometimes neglected. Improvement in cardiovascular efficiency is the one aspect most associated with general fitness programs. The heart, lungs, and blood vessels are optimally stimulated by endurance or aerobic exercise. Most experts agree that emphasizing aerobic exercise in the fitness program will produce the most beneficial changes in the most body systems. The health of the heart, lungs, and blood vessels is especially critical to the prevention of atherosclerosis, the clogging of blood vessels which causes more deaths and disability in Americans than any other disease. But cardiovascular or aerobic exercise alone may not produce the "total fitness" desired by many individuals. While aerobic training will improve the strength and function of the muscle groups used in the exercise, it generally does not produce total body muscular tone. Aerobic training, which typically uses the leg muscles, may not generate even "adequate" upper body strength. Therefore, muscular resistance training must be used to supplement the aerobic cardiovascular program.

Muscular strength and flexibility allow efficient movement during routine daily activities. In addition, muscular fitness causes enhanced sports' skill performance, decreases the likelihood of injury, and provides reserve capacity for emergencies. This type of training can be gratifying and, by improving appearance, can help a person's self image. Thus, muscular fitness is an important component of total body fitness. Many men and women have what can be called "adequate strength." But if individuals become less active as family and job responsibilities become more time-consuming, muscular function will diminish. This loss of function can be prevented with a muscular resistance training program.

The competitive athlete must achieve maximal levels of strength and power for success in most sports. Such high level muscular function can be obtained only through heavy resistance exercises. Through progressive overload training, the muscles can safely handle the stresses and demands of competitive athletics.

Perhaps no other aspect of the recent fitness boom has involved more people than resistance training. Weight rooms at high schools, colleges, and fitness centers are often filled to capacity. But resistance training must be designed to meet the goals of enhancing muscular function. In addition, it must be incorporated into a total fitness program. Seldom can muscular resistance training provide the sole exercise for total fitness achievement. Therefore, the discussions in this book will attempt to provide guidelines for incorpotating muscular resistance exercises into the total fitness program. Some discussion will be provided on "maximal" muscular improvement in relation to sports performance. However, the major emphasis will relate to safely improving muscular strength and tone without detriment to other physiological functions, especially the cardiovascular system.

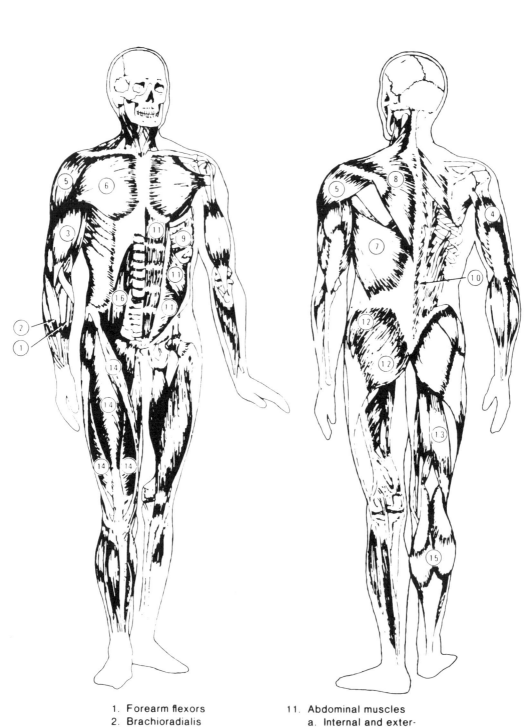

1. Forearm flexors
2. Brachioradialis
3. Biceps
4. Triceps
5. Deltoid
6. Pectoral muscles
7. Latissimus dorsi
8. Trapezius
9. Serratus anterior
10. Erector spinae
   (spinal extensors)
11. Abdominal muscles
   a. Internal and exter-
      nal obliques
   b. Rectus abdominis
   c. Transversalis
12. Gluteal muscles
13. Hamstrings
14. Quadriceps muscles
15. Gastrocnemius, soleus
   muscles
16. Iliopsoas (under ab-
   dominal muscles)

Major muscles of the body. Reproduced with permission of Cramer Products, Inc., Gardner, KS.

PRINCIPLES OF
MUSCULAR CONTRACTION

In order to understand the scientific principles which govern muscular development, it is important to first examine the way in which muscle contracts. Many components of muscle play a role in generating movement. Stimulating these components by activity causes each aspect to be developed. If some muscular components are not stimulated during movement, they will be less likely to be developed.

MUSCULAR STRUCTURE

Most muscles of the body are attached to bones by a mass of connective tissue called tendons. When the muscle shortens, it tends to pull the associated bones toward each other, and when the muscle lengthens, the bones move apart. Muscle operates at many different levels but can be divided primarily into gross structure (large) and microstructure (small). The largest functional unit is the intact muscle itself and attaching tendon (Figure 1.1). Inside

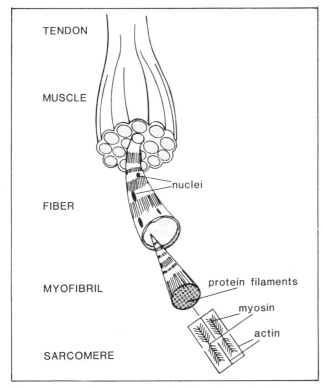

TENDON

MUSCLE

FIBER

nuclei

MYOFIBRIL

protein filaments

myosin

actin

SARCOMERE

Figure 1.1. *The structure of skeletal muscle. The components are arranged from the largest at the top of the figure to the smallest at the bottom.*

each muscle are thousands of muscle fibers. The fiber is the true cell of the muscle because it contains the nuclei, mitochondria, and other material which control and perform the biological activity of the cell. Each muscle fiber consists of thousands of myofibrils, protein structures so small they can be seen only with the aid of a microscope. Thus, the myofibrils begin the microstructure of the muscle.

The functional unit inside the myofibril is called a sarcomere. Each sarcomere contains the protein filaments actin and myosin (Figure 1.1). When myosin connects to actin and pulls, the sarcomere shortens; when many myosins in different sarcomeres pull their associated actins, many sarcomeres shorten, and thus the entire muscle moves.

Two additional proteins in the sarcomere help regulate actin and myosin interaction. These "regulatory proteins" are called troponin and tropomyosin. These regulators become associated with calcium (Ca^{++}) to signal the start of muscular contraction; their association with magnesium (Mg^+) and removal of Ca^{++} are related to muscular relaxation. These two minerals are very important to muscular function, and dietary deficiencies or losses of Ca^{++} and Mg^+ may cause muscular soreness, cramping, and other muscular disorders.

The myofibril is a primary site of muscular development. Increases in actin and myosin proteins as a consequence of muscular training cause the sarcomeres to increase in size. As a result, the many muscle fibers become larger, and the total muscle becomes larger and stronger.

Although the total muscle, muscle fiber, and sarcomere are important biological units, the most important functional unit related to physical activity is the motor unit. This is the "neuromuscular" component and consists of a nerve (motorneuron) from the central nervous system (CNS) and all the muscle fibers which the nerve "innervates" (Figure 1.2). Most muscles have at least two types of motor units: slow twitch (ST) which have smaller nerves and fast twitch (FT) which have larger nerves (Figure 1.2).

The different motor units are stimulated depending on the intensity and the speed of the

3

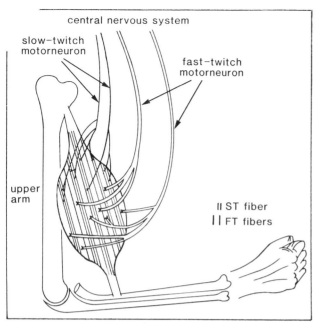

Figure 1.2. *The nerves and muscle fibers of motor units. Fast twitch (FT) motor units have larger nerves and fibers than slow twitch (ST) motor units.*

desired muscular contraction. ST motor units are required for low-intensity, slow, sustained contractions, while FT motor units are necessary for rapid, high intensity contractions.

Muscle fibers do not "volunteer" to assist with contraction; they are "recruited" by the CNS. Motor unit recruitment occurs in two ways: spatial and temporal summation. In spatial (space) recruitment, additional motor units are stimulated to help with a movement. For example, if a person is holding an empty bucket in one hand, very few motor units are necessary to sustain the contraction (Figure 1.3). However, if suddenly a large rock is put into the bucket, additional motor units are necessary to hold up the bucket. Usually the motor units recruited will be of the same fiber type, in this case ST, unless the weight is so

heavy that the FT motor units also must be recruited. In addition, as ST motor units fatigue, FT units will be recruited.

In temporal (time) recruitment, the *same* motor units are stimulated at an increased frequency of nervous activity. In this way, each motor unit which has been stimulated previously is excited to produce even greater tension (Figure 1.3). Temporal recruitment is important during maximal efforts. For example, when holding the heavy, rock-filled bucket, eventually all motor units will be stimulated. If this does not produce adequate tension to hold the bucket (or as motor units fatigue), all motor units will be stimulated with increased electrical activity of the motor neuron. Through both spatial and temporal recruitment, maximal tension can be obtained in a given muscle.

How does the CNS know which type of motor unit to recruit? The system of recruitment depends on differences in the motor neuron which innervates the different fiber types. The nerves associated with ST muscle fibers are small and "low threshold" which makes them easier to stimulate than the FT nerves (Figure 1.2). This means it takes less electrical (nervous) activity to stimulate ST motor units. These fibers are recruited when low intensity, slow muscular movements are required. On the other hand, the neurons associated with FT fibers are large and more difficult to stimulate. These are recruited during high intensity, rapid muscular contractions such as heavy weight lifting. These fibers also fatigue faster than ST fibers and thus cannot sustain the high intensity activity very long.

Thus ST motor units are always initially recruited during low intensity activity. As the loads or speed are increased, ST motor units will continue to be recruited, especially by spatial recruitment. FT motor units are recruited if the ST

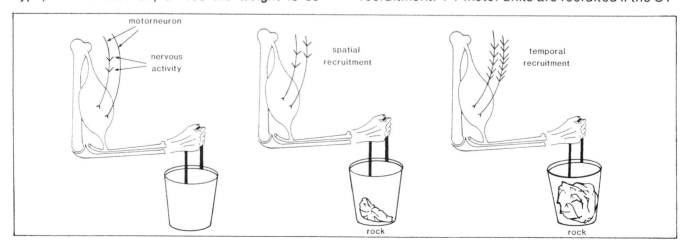

Figure 1.3. *Motor unit recruitment. Motor units are called into action by spatial and temporal recruitment. Both kinds of recruitment are necessary to lift heavy loads.*

fibers in the motor units fatigue or if the load or speed become too great for ST muscle fibers to perform the activity. At that time "heterogeneous" motor unit recruitment will occur; both ST and FT motor units will be recruited.

The recruitment system as described has some additional properties related to the motor-neuron threshold. Because the FT units require more stimulation than ST, the ST units will be activated virtually any time the FT motor units are recruited. If the contraction is rapid, the recruited ST units may participate very little in the actual muscular movement. However, this phenomenon suggests that activities which develop FT muscle fibers will also help develop ST fibers. The reverse is not true since ST recruitment will not necessarily involve FT motor units, and the carry over effect would be less likely. Only when ST fibers fatigue during sustained, low-intensity contraction, will FT motor units be recruited (spatially) to assist with the contraction.

ENERGY REQUIREMENTS

Weight training exercises generally utilize the anaerobic energy system rather than the aerobic. But certain types of circuit resistance training (CRT) can stimulate the aerobic energy production system. Thus both anaerobic and aerobic energy use may be utilized during muscular training.

Anaerobics

Anaerobics refers to high intensity, short-burst activity in which the muscles rely heavily on the production of energy without adequate oxygen. Adenosine triphosphate (ATP) is a key substrate for this high intensity activity. In addition, muscular creatine phosphate (CP) and stored carbohydrate (CHO) called glycogen are utilized to replenish ATP during intensive exercise. Virtually no blood glucose or stored fat is utilized in high intensity anaerobic exercise. Most types of lifting exercises rely primarily on anaerobic energy production. These exercises cannot be sustained for very long without rest periods because anaerobic metabolism is inefficient, and the exercising muscles generally do not tolerate the buildup of "lactic acid." This chemical is produced from the anaerobic metabolism of glycogen. Lactic acid is not the culprit it was once thought to be. It is a very usable energy source, and probably does not promote muscular soreness. It does,

however, make the muscle more acidic which reduces the activity of chemical reactions and the contractile machinery, and these problems can lead to "fatigue."

Anaerobics make the heart and cardio-vascular system work very hard. In the trained individual, this has little adverse effect and may at times be beneficial to the total physiological fitness of the individual. For the older individual, especially those out of condition, high intensity heavy lifting may do more harm than good, but using lighter weights and slower movements may be beneficial.

Anaerobic muscular exercise utilizes primarily "fast-twitch muscle fibers" (Table 1.1). At least two kinds of fast twitch fibers have been identified. Type IIb fast-twitch fibers are very adept at producing large amounts of anaerobic energy. Thus, they can work very hard for short periods of time, but Type IIb fibers fatigue relatively quickly. Type IIa fast-twitch fibers also are used in lifting work, but they have less anaerobic capacity than the IIb fibers. Even the "slow-twitch" or Type I fibers are involved in anaerobic activity. Because these motor units have a lower threshold for stimulation than fast-twitch, they are recruited in high intensity activity, such as resistance exercise, but they provide only a little help since slow-twitch fibers cannot produce large amounts of anaerobic energy. Only when the fast-twitch fibers begin to fatigue, do slow-twitch fibers play a significant role in performing resistance exercises. At this time, lifting performance declines.

Aerobics

Activities which are low enough intensity so that they can be prolonged and thus use large amounts of oxygen are called aerobics. The majority of the scientific research indicates that this type of exercise produces the most beneficial overall effects on the cardiovascular system. Aerobics depend primarily on slow-twitch fibers which are capable of producing large amounts of aerobic energy because of their numerous cellular mitochondria (Table 1.1). Fast-twitch muscle fibers are not recruited in low intensity activity until the slow-twitch muscles are very fatigued. Type IIa fibers have some aerobic capabilities and thus are able to assist to some degree late in the aerobic workout. Type IIb muscle fibers have little aerobic capacity and thus cannot sustain aerobic activity for very long. Therefore, aerobic exercise training primarily affects slow-twitch fibers, with some carry-over effect on IIa fibers, but little effect on

Table 1.1. *Basic Differences Among Muscle Fiber Types*

CHARACTERISTIC	FIBER TYPE		
	Slow-Twitch	Fast-Twitch	
	I	IIa	IIb
Animal Nonmenclature	SO*	FOG	FG
% In Typical Muscle	50	34	16
Twitch Time	Slow	Fast	Fast
Color	Red	White	White
Fatigue	Slow	Fast	Fast
Motor Neuron Size	Small	Large	Large
Stimulation Velocity	Slow	Fast	Fast
Threshold: Ease to Stimulate	Low: Easy	High: Harder	High: Harder
Aerobic Capacity	High	Medium	Low
Oxidative Enzymes	High	Medium	Low
Mitochondria Number	High	Medium	Low
Anaerobic Capacity	Low	Medium	High
Lactate Production	Low	Medium	High
Fat Stores	High	Low	Low
Glycogen	High	High	High

*SO = slow twitch oxidative   FOG = fast twitch oxidative & glycolytic   FG = fast twitch glycolytic

Reprinted with permission from T.R. Thomas, and C.J. Zebas. *Scientific Exercise Training.* Copyright © 1987 by Kendall/Hunt Publishing Co.

IIb fibers. The aerobic component of muscular workouts can be increased by using lighter weights and more repetitions with little rest between exercises. (See Chapter 10.)

Carbohydrate and Fat as Energy Sources

High intensity anaerobic activity depends on the muscular substrates ATP, CP, and glycogen which do not require oxygen to produce energy (Table 1.2). Muscular stores of ATP and CP are especially limited and thus last only for a few seconds during resistance training. In anaerobic exercise lasting longer than a few seconds, glycogen is used as a primary energy source. Likewise, in low or moderate intensity aerobic activity, ATP and CP stores provide the energy only very early in exercise. Thereafter, carbohydrate and fat must provide the fuel for the work.

Although glycogen is a very effective form of stored energy, most energy in the body is stored as fat. Fat depots in adipose tissue are located in many observable places, especially in the abdomen, seat, and thigh regions. Such depots serve as efficient energy storage because fat does not require large quantities of water in storage as does CHO. A gram of stored fat will yield 9 kilocalories (Cal) of energy while a gram of CHO will yield 4 Cal. Body fat stores probably could provide close to 75,000 Cal as energy while CHO only about 2000 Cal. Thus, the supply of CHO is relatively limited and can be depleted with prolonged exercise or in repeated vigorous workouts such as resistance exercise. On the other hand, CHO provides more energy per liter of oxygen consumed during exercise and is about 10% more efficient as an energy source than is fat. In other words, fat is more efficient in energy storage, and CHO is more efficient in energy use.

Because of this greater efficiency, CHO is often mistakenly considered the preferred energy source for all types of activity. Muscle glycogen is the most important fuel in lifting exercises and is probably used to some degree in all activities lasting longer than a few seconds. However, the extent that fat or carbohydrate is used as energy depends primarily on the intensity and duration of the exercise bout.

At rest, the body's use of fat is slightly higher than the use of CHO. The use of protein for energy is negligible except at times when CHO stores are very low such as after very prolonged exercise or in starvation. When an individual works very mildly for at least 20 minutes, fat use

Table 1.2. *Energy Sources Used in Exercise*

ANAEROBIC ACTIVITY	AEROBIC ACTIVITY
Adenosine Triphosphate (ATP)	Muscle Glycogen
Creatine Phosphate (CP)	Adipose Trigylcerides (TG)
Muscle Glycogen	Liver Glycogen and Blood Glucose
	Muscle Triglycerides

increases while the use of CHO decreases. Initially in light exercise, such as walking, stored ATP, CP and CHO are the most important energy sources. After about 20-30 minutes, fat is mobilized from adipose tissue and becomes the primary energy source. Fat is the principle energy substrate, providing up to 75% of the total energy requirement, after 30 minutes of light, continuous exercise (50% of maximal aerobic capacity, heart rate about 130 bpm). Endurance trained individuals burn more fat during exercise than untrained or weight-trained individuals.

In low-moderate intensity resistance exercise, such as circuit resistance training, carbohydrate and fat are used about equally as energy sources, especially late in the session. In higher intensity, heavy resistance lifting, the muscle's use of glycogen is increased while the use of fat is decreased (Figure 1.4). Muscle stores of ATP and CP can provide energy only for

10-20 seconds of high intensity work. In such work, muscle glycogen is a primary energy source, and lactic acid from anaerobic metabolism inhibits fat use. Lactic acid usually accumulates to some degree in most types of heavy resistance training. The extent of accumulation is less if longer rest periods (2-3 min) are used. Regardless, fat is not a primary energy source during most of the exercise session, but may be important during the rest periods late in the session and during recovery after the session (Figure 1.4).

Traditional muscular weight training utilizing heavy resistance generally causes the heart rate to reach very high levels during the exercse. The high intensity, rapid movements by the muscle causes the metabolic system to rely on ATP-CP and glycogen as energy sources. Even though the heart rate may be high, the total oxygen consumption and total caloric expenditure generally are relatively low

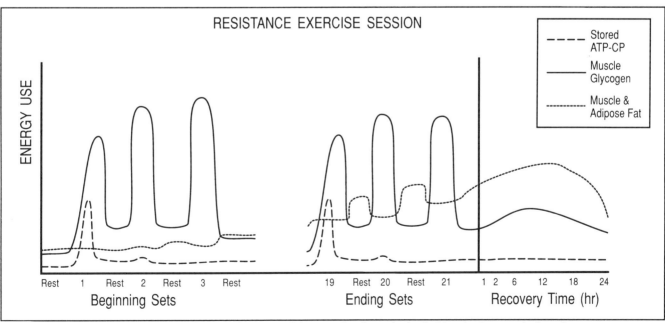

Figure 1.4. *Energy sources used during a resistance training session (hypothetical). Muscle glycogen is the primary energy source, but fat use increases during the late rest periods and during recovery. Note: Set = 8-10 RM over 1 min period. Rest = 2 min between exercises. In the initial three sets, one muscle group is used and in the final three sets, a different muscle group is used.*

during lifting exercises because of the small amount of muscle mass used for each lift. (See Chapter 4.) Muscular resistance exercises use between 5 and 10 kcal per min (kcal/min) of exercise or about 300 to 600 kcal/hour of lifting. These values may be an overestimation of the energy expenditure depending on the length of the rest periods between lifting exercises. Regardless, the *total* caloric expenditure during a muscular strength workout is approximately comparable to brisk walking, slow jogging, or moderate cycling. However, the energy sources used during the lifting exercises are quite different than during the more aerobic activities. The continuous aerobic exercises rely more heavily on fat energy. Because the use of fat in recovery from lifting and the increases in muscle mass caused by strength training, weight lifters may have a very low percentage of body fat. (See Appendix D.)

TYPES OF MUSCULAR CONTRACTION

Skeletal muscle can be stimulated to contract in a variety of different ways. Basically muscular contractions can be divided into two types: 1. static or isometric in which the internal muscular tension is equal to the external resistance and no movement occurs, 2. dynamic in which muscular tension produces movement. Dynamic contractions in which the internal muscular tension is greater than the external resistance is called "concentric." In this type of contraction, the muscle shortens and the associated bones move toward each other. In "eccentric" contractions, the internal muscular tension is less than the external resistance, and the bones move apart. The muscle is "stronger" when contracting eccentrically, and it can handle more weight in this "negative" movement than in the "positive" concentric contraction.

The understanding of concentric and eccentric contractions is very important in prescribing exercises for specific muscles. For example, in the push-up, the same muscle groups are involved in both the up-phase and the down-phase of the exercise (Figure 1.5). This exercise would be prescribed only if the goal was to strengthen the triceps or the chest muscles. It would not be a good exercise for developing the biceps or back muscles.

Another type of dynamic contraction is "isokinetic" in which the muscle moves at a specific controlled speed. This type of contraction requires an external device to alter resistance so that the speed of contraction is the

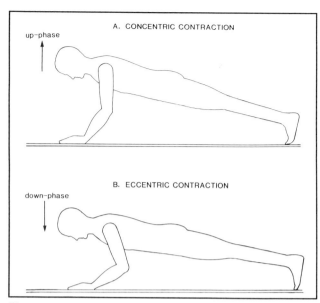

Figure 1.5. *A. Concentric and B. Eccentric muscular contractions. The same muscle groups (pectorals and triceps) control the movement in both the up and down phases of the push-up.*

same throughout the range of movement. This type of contraction may be important in exercising the muscle at high speeds, which approximate those used during physical activity and sports performance.

POWER

The development of muscular tension relative to the speed of movement is important to muscular power. Basically power is the ability to generate force very rapidly. Power = force x velocity. The development of power is based on the principle of the load-velocity curve of muscle (Figure 1.6). As the load on a muscle increases, the speed at which the muscle can contract decreases. It is easy for anyone to demonstrate this principle simply by lifting different weights (Figure 1.3). The lighter load can be lifted more rapidly. Since both load (force) and speed are components of power, the power curve can be superimposed with the load-velocity curve (Figure 1.6). On the power curve, as the load on a muscle increases, the power also increases up to a point. Eventually the load becomes so heavy that velocity of contraction is compromised too much and power decreases. Therefore, maximal power can be defined as the "optimal combination" of muscular force and velocity. Note that the optimal combination occurs at only 30-50% of the maximal load. Thus, the theory of training muscular power with lighter loads and faster movements has some scientific basis.

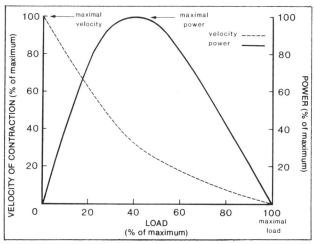

Figure 1.6. *Load-velocity and load-power relations. As the load on a muscle increases, the speed of contraction decreases. The combination of load and velocity determine muscular power.*

A common example of the load-velocity-power phenomenon is the bat selection by a baseball power hitter. A heavier bat will not necessarily produce more home runs. Rather, the bat needs to be a heavy enough load to optimize muscular velocity and maximize power. A bat which is too light will allow too little force and too much velocity; a bat which is too heavy will cause too much force development in the muscle at the expense of velocity of contraction and thus produce less than maximal power.

Baseball power hitters select a bat size based on feel and trial and error. The optimal bat load could be determined scientifically by altering the bat weight and timing the swing with an electronic timer. From these data, Figure 1.6 could be plotted for the hitter and the optimal bat weight determined.

Body weight also is an important factor in the load-velocity-power relationships. Simply gaining body weight will increase the load on specific muscles. This may or may not increase total power. For example, a long jumper may need to determine an optimal weight which maximizes power at takeoff. Likewise, simply adding body weight to the football power fullback may not increase his blocking or ball carrying power. The effect of weight gain or loss in sports depends on the effect which the load change has on velocity of contraction and maximal power.

SKELETAL LEVER SYSTEM

Many factors superimpose their effect on the internal muscular components to affect contraction. Such factors include age, sex, temperature, momentum, and skeletal structure. The latter is perhaps the most important of these extra muscular factors. It has been established that the strength capabilities within a muscle varies throughout the range of motion. (See Chapter 2.) Although the availability of actin and myosin to interact plays some role in this tension development capacity, the primary determinant of muscular strength at a given angle, is the bone and muscle lever system. Virtually every muscle has places in the range of motion where the strength capacity is high and places where this capacity is low, often called sticking points. For example, the maximal strength-generating capacity in the biceps is at a joint angle of about 100°, while the muscle is "weakest" at 180° and 40°. The joint angle is the angle that the two associated bones make with each other. At a joint angle of 90°, the forearm is parallel with the ground.

These differences in strength-generating capacities are caused primarily by the muscle tendon's angle of pull on the bone or "mechanical leverage." Another way of stating this is that a muscle tension of 100 lbs. can lift more weight at 100° joint angle than at 160° joint angle. This lever system principle also indicates natural advantages in some individuals. For example, the distance from the elbow that the biceps attaches to the arm bone (radius) in part determines the limb strength and velocity of movement. If the biceps attachment is farther from the elbow, the "force arm" is increased and a given muscular tension can lift more weight. However, the "resistance arm" would be shorter in this example, and thus the velocity of movement would be less than if the biceps attachment was closer to the elbow. This example illustrates that some individuals have a natural mechanical advantage for producing strength, while others have superior capabilities at producing limb velocity. Understanding these biomechanical principles may help to prevent discouragement if individuals in similar training programs progress differently.

SUGGESTED READINGS

1. Fox, E.L., R.W. Bowers, M.L. Foss. *Physiological Basis of Physical Education and Athletics.* Philadelphia: Saunders College, Chapters 5, 6, and 7, 1988.
2. Wescott, W.L. *Strength Fitness: Physiological Principles and Training Techniques.* Boston: Allyn and Bacon, Chapters 1 and 2, 1982.

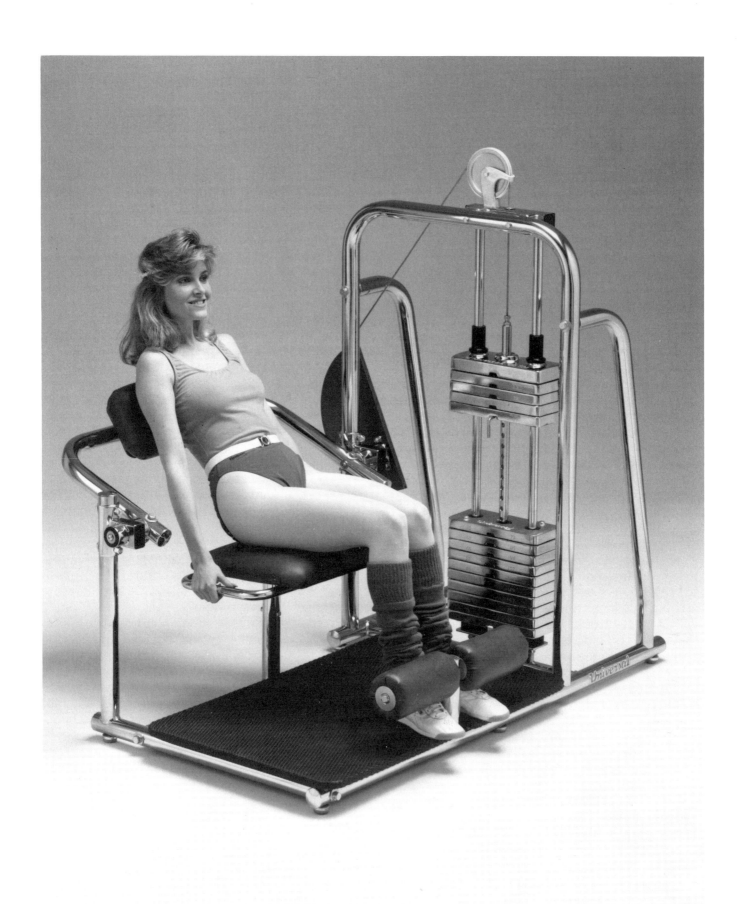

METHODS OF PROVIDING RESISTANCE FOR MUSCLE

Nearly any type of muscular activity may be beneficial in developing or maintaining the fitness of muscle. Simply raising the arms can provide a stimulus to the involved muscular components. In raising the arms over the head, the weight of the hand and arm provide the resistance for the muscles. Improvement in muscular strength and performance, however, generally requires a method of providing a greater overload resistance to stimulate the muscle to produce greater forces.

Just as there are many kinds of muscular contractions, there are a variety of ways of providing external resistance for muscular exercise. Currently the study of resistance devices is one of the most dynamic aspects of the fitness boom era. Major equipment manufactures are spending millions of dollars in developing new resistance machines. The goal of this investment is to make instruments which provide the most appropriate type of resistance for the muscle. Unfortunately, the type of resistance that is actually best for training muscle is unknown. This is an area which is being vigorously researched by exercise physiologists in the U.S. and other countries.

STATIC RESISTANCE

When resistance is unmovable, it is termed static or isometric. These terms indicate that the load is so heavy, the muscle cannot move it, and thus the muscle length remains the same during the contraction. Because static resistance provides the muscle with stress only at a specific point in the range of motion, strength gains are "angle specific." That is, the strength gained occurs in a very limited area of the working range. For example, if an individual attempted to lift a heavy desk by flexing the biceps muscle, the strength gain would be limited to the arm angle at which the contraction was performed. Of course, the elbow angle could be changed several times which would allow the muscle to be worked throughout the range. This requires a very long workout period for each muscle and generally is not feasible. Regardless, such exercises would have little relevance to the way the muscle is actually used during activity. Very few activities utilize static muscular contraction.

Another disadvantage of using static resistance is the relatively large increase in blood pressure during the exercise. In addition, the pressure in the chest, called intrathoracic pressure, also can be elevated. Both of these effects diminish the heart's ability to pump blood to the working muscles and to other organs such as the brain. These effects can be especially dangerous in the older individual. Static or isometric exercises are not recommended for most people. Many better ways exist for providing resistance to the muscle.

Static exercise can be used for brief time periods by young adults when other resistance exercises are not available (e.g., vacation). In addition, isometric instruments can be used for testing muscular strength. The cable tensiometer and hand grip and back dynomometers are examples of such testing instruments.

ISOTONIC RESISTANCE

Isotonic methods are the traditional types of weight lifting. These include the standard free-weight barbell and dumbbell as well as original weight lifting machines such as the Universal Gym. Isotonic resistance provides a "constand load" on the muscle throughout the entire range of motion. The muscle must contract with both concentric and eccentric dynamic contractions to raise and lower the weight, respectively. If the isotonic exercise is performed correctly, the muscle is stressed throughout its complete contraction range. Since the muscle is "stronger" when performing eccentrically, it is less overloaded during this phase of the exercise. In addition, constant resistance exercises do not tax each joint angle equally. Remember that the skeletal lever system causes the muscle to be stronger at certain angles. Therefore, at points where the muscle is strongest, the weight will tax it less than at points where the muscle is weakest (Figure 2.1). For example, in the biceps curl, a 100 lb. barbell might cause the muscle to develop maximal tension at 180° and 45° joint

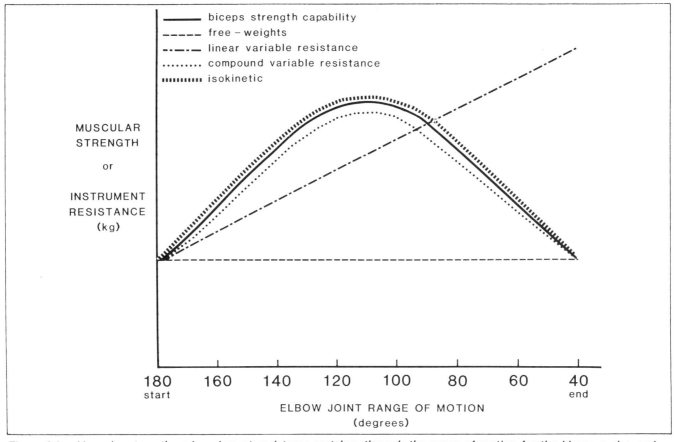

Figure 2.1. *Muscular strength and equipment resistance matchup through the range of motion for the biceps curl exercise. Adapted from T.R. Thomas. Muscular training.* Scholastic Coach *53: September, 1983.*

angles (beginning and end of the lift). But at 100° joint angle, the muscle is not taxed as much. This constant resistance technique may cause some points in the range of motion to develop greater strength gains than others. This selective improvement may be beneficial in that the weaker points might catch up to the stronger points in the contraction range. On the other hand, constant resistance training may be a disadvantage since the strongest points in the range may not develop to their full capacity.

Momentum or inertia of the weight also is altered from the start of the lift to the end, and this changes the load which the muscle feels through the range of motion. This is one reason why free-weight exercise is traditionally performed at slow speeds in an attempt to lessen the effect of momentum. Some of the variable resistance and isokinetic machines which do not use weight stacks, have eliminated the effect of inertia on the resistance.

Barbell free-weights require both the dominant and non-dominant limbs to share the load equally. Thus, muscular balance between the two sides of the body is better maintained. In addition, free-weight lifting requires balancing the bar in many directions and not just the direction of the lift. This may require additional beneficial muscular activity during the exercise. These potential advantages of free-weights are countered by the greater skill required to perform free-weight exercises than machine exercises. Increased danger of losing control and even dropping the weights are potential for the novice. A partner also is required for spotting on some lifts. Because of these potential problems, use of free-weight, constant-resistance exercises require appropriate training and supervision. Heavy free-weight lifting is recommended only for experienced weight lifters with the primary goal of maximizing muscular bulk and body muscular balance.

VARIABLE RESISTANCE

The newest and commercially most competitive area of resistance equipment is the development of variable resistance machines. With this equipment, the resistance is altered throughout the range of motion in an attempt to match the changing capabilities of muscle at different joint angles (Figure 2.1). Many techniques have been devised to alter resistance during the range of motion. One of the first methods was developed by Nautilus, which

Figure 2.2. *Nautilus shoulder press. The variable resistance cams are shown behind the shoulder and seat of the exercise. Photo was provided by Nautilus Sports/Medical Industries, Inc.*

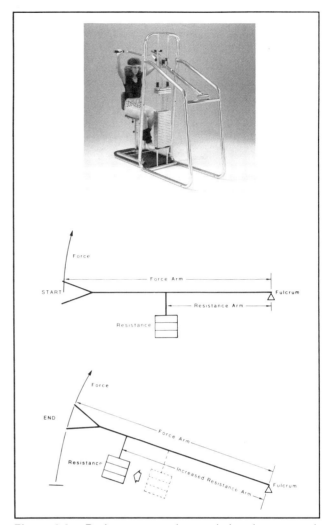

Figure 2.3. *Resistance arm change during the concentric phase of the lift in the Universal Centurion shoulder press. The resistance increases through the concentric phase range of motion and decreases through the eccentric phase. Inset photo was provided by Universal Gym Equipment, Inc.*

used a "nautilus shell" shaped cam to alter the load. In this system, as the pulley cord is moved around the cam, the resistance arm distance is altered and thus the resistance felt by the muscle is changed throughout its range. (Figure 2.2). Such a cam potentially allow the resistance to be increased at the strongest points in the movement range and decreased at the weakest points, thus a "compound resistance" change.

Another novel system, developed by Universal, mechanically alters the load by physically moving the weights to change the resistance arm length (Figure 2.3). Such a system causes the resistance to continually increase throughout the concentric phase of the range of motion, and decrease during the eccentric phase. These are "linear resistance" changes. In the example of the biceps curl, the resistance some-what matches the muscular strength early in the lift but overshoots the muscle capabilities late in the lift (Figure 2.1). Momentum allows the lift to be completed. Universal also has machines with compound cam, e.g., on the leg extension (Chapter 10).

Other examples of innovative mechanisms which produce variable resistance include the Soloflex resistance bands or weight straps. As

these straps are stretched through the concentric range of motion, the resistance is increased (Figure 2.4). In Keiser strength equipment, muscular movement causes an engine-like piston to compress air in a pneumatic cylinder, thus increasing the resistance through the range-of-motion. A built-in system of linkages attached to the machine also adjusts the resistance (Figure 2.5). The Hydra-Fitness exercise machines alter resistance with hydraulic cylinders in which hydraulic fluid provides the resistance for concentric contractions only (Figure 2.6). See Chapter 10 for additional illustrations and descriptions of the various machines.

Additional resistance systems are being developed at a rapid pace. Each has a different mechanism attempting to match resistance with muscular function. The success of these

Figure 2.4. *Soloflex shoulder press. Stretched weight straps are shown on the vertical stand. Photo was provided by Soloflex, Inc.*

Figure 2.6. *Hydra-Fitness shoulder press/lat pull. Hydraulic cylinders are shown on the front of the instrument. Photo was provided by Hydra-Fitness Industries.*

Figure 2.5. *Keiser shoulder press. Air cylinder is shown behind the back. Photo was provided by Keiser Sports Health Equipment.*

strategies may depend on how well an individual's strength curve of a given muscle matches the specific resistance curve of the machine.

Although certain systems seem to have theoretical advantage, very little research has examined the muscular strength – machine resistance match-ups of the various types of strength equipment. Current scientific findings do not support the use of any one type of variable resistance mechanism. Rather, all systems seem to improve muscular strength. The development of various training devices seems beneficial since nearly anyone interested in muscular training can find equipment which suits him/her. The selection of one variable resistance system over another then may relate to the specific goals of an individual. For example, some machines are easier to work at higher speeds than others. This is especially true with machines which do not utilize actual weights which increase momentum. In addition, the range for the various equipment.

ISOKINETIC RESISTANCE

Another kind of muscular training which uses a form of variable resistance is isokinetic

14

exercises. In this "same speed" technique, the movement speed is set on a dial. This is the key distinguishing characteristic of true isokinetic equipment. Speed of the instrument is selected and not the amount of resistance. The machine allows the movement to proceed no faster than the set speed no matter how much tension is produced in the contracting muscle. By this mechanism, an exact resistance can be matched to the force capabilities of the muscle (Figure 2.1). If a maximal effort is attempted at all joint angles, the machine resistance is maximal at all joint angles. The advantage of such a machine is to optimally tax the muscle throughout the range of motion. Isokinetic resistance training involves no eccentric contraction, only concentric. This may be beneficial since eccentric movements have been associated with muscular soreness. However, the lack of eccentric training also may be a disadvantage since most sports activities require eccentric contractions. For example, the rapid bending of the knees to lower the torso in making a tennis stroke or gathering for a jump shot or spike, all require eccentric contractions of the quadriceps muscles.

One of the first popular isokinetic devices was developed by Mini-Gym. The equipment provided an inexpensive, simple method of isokinetic resistance for a limited number of muscle groups. An updated Mini-Gym device is illustrated in Figure 2.7. Cybex by Lumex, a noteworthy isokinetic testing instrument has a recording of the performance which is valuable in muscular function testing (Figure 2.8). The major advantage of isokinetic exercise is the ability to train at high speeds and thus develop the force and speed aspects of power. Most individuals lift weights at 60-100 degrees/sec. Many power events (e.g., jumping and sprinting) are performed at speeds two to three times greater than this. Previous research indicates that "performance power" is improved only when muscle is trained at speeds equal to or greater than the performance speed. If this principle is true, athletes using traditional weight training techniques may not be improving muscle function at speeds necessary for elite sports performance.

A major disadvantage of isokinetic muscular training is that the resistance of the machine is solely dependent upon the user's motivation. The effort can be minimal, maximal, or somewhere in-between. The instrument controls only the speed of movement. Because of the potential for "cheating," isokinetic exercise, in the present form, may not achieve its

Figure 2.7. Mini-Gym isokinetic instrument.

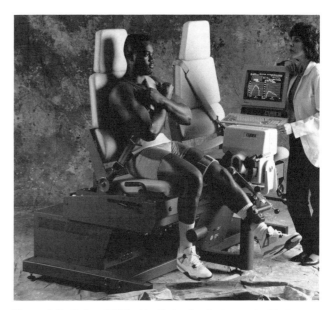

Figure 2.8. Cybex 350 isokinetic testing instrument. Photo was provided by Cybex.

15

theoretical capabilities as a training tool. Some coaches and athletic trainers have questioned the appropriateness of isokinetic training since the muscle seldom performs isokinetically during normal activities. In addition, the device provides resistance only when the speed of the lift equals the set machine speed. During the initial phases of the exercise, as the muscle accelerates to the set speed, no resistance is encountered. Therefore, the resistance is not maximal through the initial range of motion, especially at fast movement settings.

Studies comparing isotonic, variable resistance, and isokinetic muscular training methods have not been conclusive. However, some studies have suggested greater gains can be obtained with isokinetic training in highly motivated individuals. All types of muscular training have been shown to produce strength gain if the workload is heavy. Whether all methods will improve muscular power is unknown.

RESISTANCE WITHOUT EQUIPMENT

Many techniques can be utilized to develop skeletal muscle fitness without the use of weight equipment. Most of these methods rely on part or all of the body weight to provide the resistance during the exercise. While these techniques may not be as effective as machine training in developing maximal muscular strength and bulk, they are very adequate in improving general muscular fitness.

Body Weight Exercises

Many common exercises require the muscles to lift the body weight off the floor. These activities require dynamic muscular contractions, both concentric and eccentric. The sit-up, push-up, and pull-up are examples of these activities. (See Chapter 10 for illustrations.) Running or jumping also are body weight lifting exercises which stress specific muscles and can be used to improve muscular fitness. One limitation to such activities can be the difficulty in exercising opposite muscle groups to maintain muscular balance (e.g., quadriceps and hamstrings).

Body weight activities generally are sufficient to maintain muscular strength and improve muscular tone. With the addition of weights to the body or by increasing the resistance with a partner, strength improvements also may be observed. (See Chapter 10.)

Plyometrics

One method of increasing the effectiveness of body weight resistance is plyometric activity. In this method, an individual jumps from a height of 12-24" and then immediately springs upward in a vertical jump. This leg training technique is based on two principles: 1) The drop-jump causes an eccentric contraction in the thigh (quadriceps) and calf (gastrocnemius) muscles. This movement causes a substantial amount of "elastic energy" to be stored in the stretched muscle. The elastic energy is used in the subsequent upward (concentric) movement. This mechanism could be visualized as a rubber-band effect. When the muscle is vigorously stretched, it has energy which wants to propel it back to its original length, like a stretched rubber band. The rubber-band effect assists the muscles in propelling the body upward in the vertical jump. 2) The drop-jump vigorously stretches the quadriceps and gastrocnemius muscles which activates the stretch reflex. The end effects of this reflex are a vigorous contraction of these same muscles plus the smaller spindle muscles producing added force of contraction. For a description of the stretch reflex during the jump, see Chapter 5.

Plyometric training can increase leg muscular power and the height of the vertical jump. However, this type of vigorous exercise can cause injury and should be used only by athletes who specifically require improved jumping or sprinting ability. This type of exercise generally is not a necessary component of the general muscular fitness program.

SUGGESTED READINGS

1. Fox, E.L. and D.K. Mathews. *The Physiological Basis of Physical Education and Athletics.* Philadelphia: Saunders College Publishing, Chapter 7, 1988.
2. Fleck, S.J. and W.J. Kraemer. Resistance training: basic principles (part 1). *Physician and Sportsmedicine.* 16:160-171, March, 1988.
3. Powers, S.K. and E.T. Howley. *Exercise Physiology: Theory and Application to Fitness and Performance.* Dubuque: Wm. C. Brown, Chapters 8 and 21, 1990.
4. Riley, D.P. *Maximum Muscular Fitness Strength Training Without Equipment.* West Point: Leisure Press, 1982.

PRINCIPLES FOR MUSCULAR RESISTANCE TRAINING

The ability of the muscles to contract forcefully and rapidly is an underlying prerequisite for successful performance in most physical activities. Many individuals underestimate the value of muscular fitness even in performing routine, daily activities. Walking, stair climbing, housework, etc. can be performed even by very weak individuals. However, these and other activities become much more efficient and less demanding when adequate muscular fitness is present. Even more demanding jobs such as opening the garage door or mowing the lawn are easier to handle with proper muscular strength. Thus, muscular training need not be reserved for athletes and body builders, but can be incorporated into any general fitness program. Certainly the techniques used by power athletes are different than those of the general fitness public. Still, many of the principles governing muscular training are relevant regardless of the training objectives.

GENERAL TERMINOLOGY

Strength is the ability of muscular contraction to exert a force either to move an object (dynamic) or against a fixed object (static). This capacity is traditionally measured with a maximal lift or tensiometer/dynomometer. Relative endurance is the ability to persist at a given submaximal task. For example, a person lifts as many times as possible a weight which represents 50% of his/her maximal strength.

Power refers to the muscle's ability to exert a force over a time period. Power can be improved either by increasing the force (strength training) or decreasing the time of movement. This latter element often is neglected in many sports training programs.

Muscular training is based on the principle of "overload" in which the muscle must perform more work than it is accustomed to doing. It is important that the overload occurs through the full range of motion since the muscle gains strength only in the movement range which it is worked. In addition, the overload must be progressive, i.e., the resistance increased periodically. Overloading a muscle generally causes the breakdown of muscular components, especially protein. This protein degradation stimulates the muscle to rebuild the sarcomeres and actually increase the amount of protein in the muscle fiber. Energy reservoirs of ATP-CP and glycogen used during exercise also are replenished in the rebuilding process. This rebuilding process is termed "supercompensation" and generally occurs over a 24 to 48 hour period following a vigorous resistance training workbout. Thus, the muscle becomes larger and stronger.

Muscular Hypertrophy

Increased muscle size is called hypertrophy, and protein (actin, myosin, enzymes) in the myofibrils is the main constituent of this process; however, increased blood capillaries, connective tissue, and substrates (ATP, CP, glycogen) also are involved.

Muscular hypertrophy is associated with rigorous strength training in which very heavy weights are used. In general, the heavier the weights used, the greater the strength and bulk gains. There are limitations to this general principle, and it is possible to use too much resistance. Generally isokinetic training is not as effective in producing hypertrophy as heavy resistance isotonic training. Testosterone is necessary for the protein synthesis associated with heavy weight training. Because women have less of this hormone than men, the female is less likely to gain large muscle bulk. Likewise, the prepubescent boy, would not be expected to develop similar muscular hypertrophy as the late adolescent or adult male.

Resistance Workout Terms

In traditional weight training terms, a "repetition" is moving the resistance through one complete range of motion and returning to the starting position (Table 3.1). The amount of resistance or weight which requires a single maximal contraction is called a one repetition maximum (1 RM). This feat indicates the maximal strength of a specific muscle or group of muscles. The amount of resistance which can be lifted only twice is called a 2 RM, and so on. A training "set" is a single series of multiple repetitions. For example, an individual may perform a 6 RM exercise in each of two sets for a total of 12 repetitions.

Table 3.1. *Resistance Workout Terminology*

Term	Definition
repetition	Moving a resistance through one complete range of motion and returning.
one repetition maximum (1 RM)	The amount of resistance which can be moved only one time through the range of motion and returned.
set	A single series of repetitions.
rest period	The time between sets.
work period	The time during which the repetitions are performed.

STRENGTH AND POWER TRAINING

Muscular Strength

Strength is best increased by exerting near maximal forces a few times each workout, i.e., high resistance, low repetition exercises. Typically the resistance is 70-85% of 1 RM with four to eight repetitions to failure (4-8 RM). Early research using untrained men and traditional free-weight training indicated that three sets of six RM on alternative days produced the greatest increments in dynamic strength. Some research evidence suggests that three sets are optimal and five sets produce no greater increase in strength. Supercompensation, the muscular rebuilding process, probably requires 24-48 hours. This process is longer after most intense, heavy exercise than after light lifting. In addition, supercompensation may take less time in well-trained individuals. The time period necessary for muscular rebuilding, therefore, dictates that alternate day workouts using the same muscle group are likely to be the most effective. Since most research dealing with dynamic strength training has utilized untrained men, it is unknown if the repetitions, sets, and frequency principles apply to well-trained individuals. Athletes and coaches have sometimes questioned the results of research which used non-athletes. Indeed, strength training research has not always produced results observed by ardent weight lifters. Athletes and other experienced lifters use a variety of heavy resistance programs apparently with good success. This supports the concept that maximal motor unit recruitment, regardless of the techniques, is a key to muscular strength gains.

Lifting speed does not seem to be important in the development of muscular strength. When using weights, fast speeds should not be attempted due to the risk of injury and the increased use of momentum in the exercise, which tends to reduce the tension required by the muscle. Likewise, the time between sets does not appear critical to the amount of strength gains. Usually trial and error is used by experienced lifters to determine the rest period. Rests of one to three minutes have been suggested for heavy resistance training.

Power

Muscular power can be enhanced in two ways: 1. increasing muscular strength, 2. increasing the speed of movement. Most traditional weight programs rely solely on increasing strength. However, with the modern types of equipment, high speed training with moderate resistance is becoming more popular. High speed training, allows the muscle to perform at contraction velocities and loads more similar to those required during the activity. This is especially true for power athletes such as the long jumper, football halfback, and volleyball spiker. This type of training allows both aspects of power: strength and speed, to be trained simultaneously. Scientific support for this technique is accumulating. Some evidence suggests that high speed isokinetic training is very effective in improving performance in motor activities such as jumping and throwing. Whether high speed muscular training is the optimal technique for successful sports' performance is unknown.

Specificity of Muscular Training

The specificity of muscular training is a vital principle for those who use weight training to improve performance in a specific activity. This principle implies that the muscle must be exercised during training in the same way it will be used in the activity. Table 3.2 indicates the different types of training specificity. It is desirable that the training duplicate the actual activity as nearly as possible.

The specificity of training principle requires careful examination of the activity and planning of the training exercises. For example, the tennis player who wishes to strengthen the forehand must determine the major muscles used (pectoralis, deltoid, triceps, wrist flexors), how they are contracting (concentric power), and the primary energy systems (ATP-CP, glycogen). The strength training exercises must incorporate each of these specific muscles and muscle functions into the program (See Chapter 10).

The specificity of training principle is not so critical for individuals who use resistance training as part of the general fitness program. When muscular training is used as a supplement to a cardiovascular fitness program or for muscular fitness and tone, the total body musculature should be utilized in the resistance training. Specific muscle groups need not be emphasized except for specific sport goals.

Muscular Endurance Training

Muscular endurance is best improved by moving a submaximal resistance as many times as possible. That is, low resistance (25 to 50% of maximum) is used with many repetitions. The use of traditional resistance training as a means of obtaining endurance generally is not very effective. Not only are such workouts very time consuming, but other forms of activity such as distance running, swimming, and cycling produce superior results. Most of the popular "endurance" programs (e.g., 2-3 sets of 12-20 RM) are actually providing better muscular strength training than endurance. These programs do increase strength and when performed in a circuit can even produce small increases in aerobic capacity. On the other hand, high speed, 30 sec isokinetic workouts may enhance "anaerobic endurance." Such improvement may be valuable in longer anaerobic events such as wrestling and middle distance running.

Muscular Balance

Research studies in sports medicine suggest that "muscular balance" is very important in preventing muscular injury as well as in enhancing success in certain athletic events. Most of the information regarding muscular

---

Table 3.2. *Types of Resistance Training Specificity*

Level	Implication: *Example*
1. Muscle and Joint Movement	The movement of the joint during the training exercise is the same as during activity. pitcher - weighted throwing
2. Specific Muscles	The muscles used in the activity are emphasized in the training program. rebounder-quadriceps, gastrocnemius
3. Muscular Function	The strength and speed requirements are the same for the training exercise and the activity. long jumper - high speed lifting
4. Energy System	The energy sources used are the same during the training as during the activity. sprinter - plyometrics (ATP-CP)

balance has been obtained by testing the leg muscles. It has been suggested that the hamstrings in the back of the leg should be at least 60% as strong as the quadriceps in the front of the *same leg* when tested at slow speeds, 60 to 120 degrees per second (°/sec).

$$\frac{\text{hamstrings strength}}{\text{quadriceps strength}} \times 100 > 60\%$$

When tested at faster speeds of 180°/sec or greater, the hamstrings strength becomes closer in magnitude to the quadriceps and at 300°/sec approaches 85-90%. Thus, when the legs are tested at speeds which more closely correspond to sports performance rates, the strength between the two muscle groups approaches equality.

$$\frac{\text{hamstring strength}}{\text{quadriceps strength}} \,(\text{at} > 180°/\text{sec}) \times 100 > 80\%$$

The two hamstring muscles (right and left) should be nearly equal or exhibit no more than 10% difference in strength or power at any testing speed. The same is true for the two quadriceps muscle groups.

$$\frac{\text{weak hamstrings}}{\text{strong hamstrings}} \times 100 > 90\%$$

$$\frac{\text{weak quadriceps}}{\text{strong quadriceps}} \times 100 > 90\%$$

Tests of muscular balance is most accurately performed isokinetically on devices such as the Cybex (See Chapter 2). If the leg muscles are not in balance, the susceptibility to leg injury is higher. In addition, successful performance is less likely, especially in competitive sprinting and jumping.

It is not known whether muscular balances in other parts of the body are as important as leg balance. However, an effort should be made to work antagonistic or opposite muscle groups in the training program. For example, triceps exercises should be combined with biceps exercises. Chest exercises should be performed with exercises for the back muscles. It may be tempting to concentrate solely on triceps strength exercises to help improve skills such as the volleyball spike and the basketball shot since this is the primary arm muscle involved. But complete neglect of the biceps can cause muscular imbalance to develop which may detrimentally affect the skill and increase the risk of injury. Some research indicates that antagonistic muscles are active during movements of the agonist and thus gain some benefit. For example,

during the biceps curl, the triceps are active as a stabilizer and therefore benefit from the exercise. These findings imply that it may not be necessary spend equal amounts of time on agonist and antagonist muscles. Rather, the primary moves of the event or sport should be emphasized.

In the general fitness program it is important to lift with opposing muscle groups. Isolating specific muscles may not be as important as in athletic weight training. Simply spending equal time using muscles in the front and back of each limb and front and back of the torso should be sufficient.

It is important to make the weaker side work as hard or harder during the exercise as the stronger side. If a double limb machine is used for the training, concentration is necessary to ensure the weak limb is working adequately. Single limb exercises may be necessary to increase the performance of the weaker side or weaker muscle group.

MUSCULAR TONE

The majority of fitness conscious Americans use muscular training for aesthetic purposes. That is, they desire to develop a leaner, stronger appearance. Muscular tone requires two processes: 1. the strengthening and hypertrophying of muscle, 2. the loss of superficial body fat. The use of strength exercises to tone a specific area of the body is called "spot reducing." Nearly all types of strength training exercises will strengthen muscle and cause it to increase in size. Moderate changes in strength and lean body weight can occur with resistances as light as 40-50% of maximum using 10-15 repetitions. Although greater hypertrophy occurs with the use of heavier weights, the ligher loads are recommended for muscular toning in the general fitness program.

Whether resistance exercises will cause the loss of superficial (under the skin) body fat is controversial. Some scientific evidence supports the theory that resistance exercises such as sit-ups and circuit weight training will decrease fat cells in the exercised area and reduce total body percent fat. If fat loss does occur in muscular training, it will be minimal. Greater body fat losses can be expected from vigorous, routine aerobic exercises. Weight-bearing activities (walking, jogging, rope jumping) are especially effective. Prolonged aerobic exercise (>20 min) promotes the mobilization of fat from body depots and the utilization of fat by muscle (See Chapter 1). Fat is mobilized from at least three areas in order of importance:

1. seat (gluteal) 2. stomach (abdomen) 3. thigh (femoral). The mobilization seems to occur in this particular order. That is, theoretically, it will be most difficult to lose fat from the thigh region and easiest to lose fat from the seat region. Stomach fat is a good energy source for exercise but not as good as the seat fat. Regardless, a substantial period of time is required to lose fat in a given area (See Chapter 7).

In summary, a degree of muscular tone can be achieved with resistance exercises. Optimal means of achieving total body tone is the combination of resistance training with aerobic conditioning.

RESISTANCE TRAINING AND CARDIOVASCULAR FITNESS

Utilizing resistance training as a means of conditioning the cardiovascular system generally is ineffective. Traditional forms of heavy resistance training produce virtually no improvement in cardiovascular efficiency. In some types of circuit resistance training, small cardiovascular benefits can be obtained. However, circuit training itself is not an adequate program for development of optimal cardiorespiratory fitness.

Circuit resistance training is a series of lifting exercises of 12-15 repetitions each using moderate weights of about 50% maximum. Minimal rest (15-30 seconds) is taken between stations. In this way, the heart rate is kept elevated and the cardiovascular system is taxed. Circuit resistance training can provide an alternative activity during times when injuries prevent aerobic training. Appropriate circuit training has been shown to maintain cardiovascular fitness and thus can be used as a short-term substitute for aerobic exercise. In any resistance training or aerobic program, static stretching should be used before and after the activity to maintain flexibility of the muscles and joints.

MUSCULAR SORENESS

The pain and discomfort associated with physical exercise usually can be prevented. Starting with light resistance workouts is one means of prevention. A second is to progress slowly from workout to workout, increasing the resistance only slightly each week. Routine stretching of the working muscle before, during, and after the workout also can prevent soreness. Other practices of comfortable exercise are listed in Table 3.3.

Table 3.3. *Considerations for Effective Exercise*	
Variable	**Practice**
progression	start mildly, progress slowly with exercise intensity and duration
stretching	static, using active muscles, before and after activity
warm-up	mild intensity at beginning of exercise session
cool-down	progressively declining intensity at end of exercise session
stitch-in-the-side	empty stomach, stretch upper torso, warm-up
breathing	natural, rhythmic, no breath-holding
time to exercise	empty stomach, before meals, after sleep not before
clothing	proper shoes, cotton socks and shirt, nylon shorts

Reprinted with permission from T.R. Thomas and C.J. Zebas. *Scientific Exercise Training.* Copyright © 1984 by Kendall/Hunt Publishing Co.

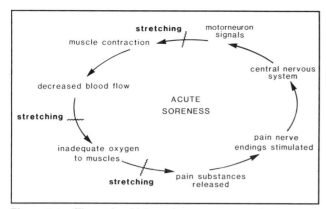

Figure 3.1. *The cycle which produces acute muscular soreness. Stretching exercises can be used to break the cycle.*

Table 3.4.	*Location of damage in muscular soreness*
Site	**Biochemical Marker**
fiber membrane	creatine kinase
contractile protein	3-methylhistidine
connective tissue	hydroxyproline

Muscular soreness can be classified as type types: 1. acute, 2. delayed. "Acute soreness" occurs during or immediately after the workout. The pain may be sharp and involve muscles spasms. This acute soreness is thought to be caused by "ischemia" or a lack of blood flow in the muscle. This creates a "hypoxia" or lack of oxygen which causes an increase in the release of substances, including lactic acid which stimulate pain endings in the muscle. The pain causes a reflex which further stimulates the muscle to contract and a painful cycle develops (Figure 3.1). Muscular stretching seems to be very effective in preventing and alleviating this cycle. Stretching should be performed before and immediately after each workout and during the workout if tightness or pain develop. It may be advantageous to continue stretching the sore muscle periodically for several hours after the workout. (See Chapter 5.)

Delayed onset muscular soreness (DOMS) can be more serious because it may indicate tissue damage. This pain develops 24-72 hours after exercise and is caused by temporary injury to the muscle or the connective tissue (tendons and sheaths). The injury stimulates an inflammatory reaction which involves the release of prostaglandins, hormones which affect many cellular reactions. One of these hormones PE2 stimulates proteolysis while another PF2 alpha stimulates protein synthesis. Thus, the injury associated with soreness also stimulates repair and rebuilding. Table 3.4 presents the sites of cell injury and markers for the determining the specific location. In other words, physicians and researchers can measure these marker compounds in blood or urine and identify which particular part of the muscle is injured. These markers may stay elevated for several days after the exercise.

Eccentric contractions, the return movement in most lifting exercises, are associated with more frequent occurrence of DOMS. These types of movements place greater stress on the muscle fiber, especially at the Z discs of the sarcomere. Cellular disruption and degradation can be extensive following eccentric contractions. Therefore, care should be taken during eccentric movements early in the training program. DOMS frequently occurs in individuals who attempt to handle too much resistance at the beginning of a training program. In addition, other exercises which require extensive eccentric actions, such as running downhill or down steps, should be avoided until the muscles are used to activity. Habituation with concentric contractions for just a few days helps prevent DOMS. Therefore, use of concentric-only machines or partner assistance with the eccentric phase during the early stages of training generally will prevent DOMS.

Unlike acute soreness, DOMS generally is not alleviated or prevented by static stretching. Rest, mild activity, and ice are effective in treating DOMS. Cooling the affected area can increase the range of motion and stimulate healing by reducing inflammation and spasms (Figure 3.2).

Figure 3.2. *Ice wrap used in the treatment for delayed-onset muscle soreness. Photo was provided by Dura*Kold, 1117 Cornell Parkway, Oklahoma City, OK 73108.*

MUSCULAR DETRAINING

Detraining

No matter how consistent the exercise habit becomes, the training regimen may get interrupted due to illness, injury, vacation, etc. Several important concepts relate to a layoff from the training program. The extent of muscular fitness loss during a layoff is less if substantial previous training has occurred. That is, once a fitness base has been established, it is more difficult to lose the enhanced muscular function (Figure 3.3). Interruptions which occur early in the training program are very detrimental and can cause the complete loss of the strength gains.

The exact timing of muscular fitness loss during a layoff is unknown. However, it seems that little loss occurs within four weeks, and then the loss is more dramatic. It is likely that a substantial percentage of the strength gains will be present even after 18 months of layoff.

Maintenance of Muscular Function

Once a muscular fitness base has been developed, "maintenance" of this level is relatively easy. That is, development of muscular fitness is more difficult than maintenance (Figure 3.3). This concept can be especially important in athletic training. Many conditioning programs for athletes require that heavy resistance training occurs in the off-season.

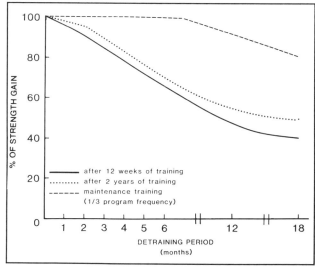

Figure 3.3. *The loss of muscular strength due to a layoff or detraining period. Strength gained from a previous resistance training program can be maintained with a strength program of only one-third the frequency.*

During the actual sport season, this strength training stops. Figure 3.3 illustrates that with complete lack of resistance training, some of the gains previously developed can be lost by mid-season. However, a lifting routine equal to only about one-third the time commitment of the rigorous off-season training generally can maintain all of the previous strength gains.

The maintenance principle is very important to both the athlete and the individual interested in general fitness. In athletics, it means resistance workouts must be incorporated into in-season training. Fortunately, this component need occur only once or twice per week, as long as the program intensity (loads) is maintained. By using little actual time in the weightroom, athletes can maintain off-season strength gains through the entire season.

In general fitness, the person need not be concerned with indefinite "progressive overload." Once adequate amounts of strength and tone have been gained, a maintenance program can be used for resistance exercise, and additional time spent in cardiovasular or alternative activities. It is probably not healthy for the muscles to continually get stronger and bigger through progressive resistance. A maintenance routine prevents staleness and allows greater gains to be made in total fitness.

BREATHING DURING RESISTANCE EXERCISES

One of the most important principles related to safe resistance training is breathing during each phase of the lift. Breathing keeps the air passages open which prevents the dramatic pressure buildup that can occur in the chest during straining exercise. Closing the air passages during a lift induces a reflex called the Valsalva maneuver in which the blood flow into the heart is reduced and the heart must pump against a greater resistance and blood pressure is increased (Figure 3.4). The idea of holding the breath during the lift to maintain torso stability may be correct mechanically, but this practice simply puts too much strain on the heart and vascular system.

Although most scientists agree on the importance of breathing, some controversy exists regarding the timing of exhalation and inhalation. There are two physiologies to consider: breathing muscles and the heart. Inhalation is an active muscular process requiring more chest muscle activity than exhalation. Since the exercising muscle is strongest in the eccentric (lowering) phase, this easier phase of contraction for the lifting muscles should be associated with the hardest phase of breathing for the respiratory muscles-inhalation. On the other hand, chest (intrathoracic) pressure increases during exhalation which increases the force of the heart necessary to eject blood. Using this heart physiological process as a guide, the eccentric muscular contraction of the lift should be associated with the hardest phase for the heart-exhalation. Unfortunately, chest muscle and heart activities suggest opposite sequences for breathing. Therefore, physiologically the exhalation-inhalation sequence probably is not critical, and comfort or desires can be used as a guide for breathing. Most experienced heavy lifters inhale during the eccentric phase and exhale during the concentric phase. But more important is simply the act of exchanging air during each phase of the lift. In the general muscular fitness program, coupling the eccentric phase with exhalation and the concentric phase with inhalation is probably better for the heart.

During high speed lifting, inhalation and exhalation may not be possible for each repetition. Rather than increasing the rate and breathing very shallow, it may be more beneficial to complete the entire repetition for each breathing phase. That is, inhale during a repetition (concentric and eccentric phases) and exhale during the next complete repetition. In this way, hyperventilation associated with rapid breathing can be avoided.

Breathing also must be stressed outside the weight room. Resistance exercises such as sit-ups and push-ups as well as shoveling dirt or chopping wood require the exchange of air during the maneuver. Once again, breath-holding should be avoided. This will require some practice at first since most individuals habitually hold the breath during these types of exercises.

POTENTIALLY DANGEROUS EXERCISE

Heavy resistance exercise itself can be potentially dangerous, especially in older individuals. Untrained men and women over 40 years of age should have fitness tests and medical clearance before undertaking a systematic exercise program, especially if it involves resistance exercises.

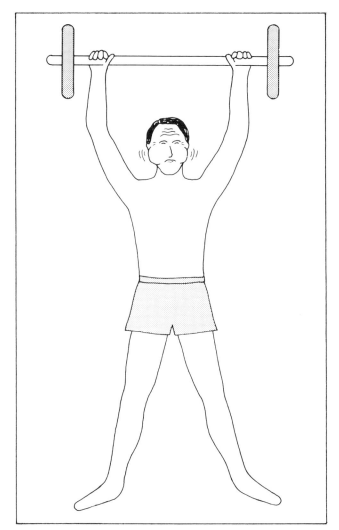

Figure 3.4. *Breath-holding during resistance exercise can be dangerous to your health.*

Exercise in the Cold

External factors coupled with heavy lifting exercises can enhance injury risk. For example, exercise in the cold is not recommended for all individuals. Cardiac patients and the elderly should seek a physician's advice about such activity. Cold can stimulate the constriction of blood vessels causing the heart to work harder and can decrease the flow of blood to some vital organs, such as the heart and brain. Vigorous arm work, such as snow shoveling, can be especially dangerous in cold weather. Small muscle exercise has a decreased mechanical and metabolic efficiency compared to large muscle exercise with the legs. In addition, isometric or static muscular contraction can occur when straining against a heavy load. Contraction with little or no movement increases the blood flow resistance against which the heart must work. As the heart

24

pumps harder it causes a disproportionate rise in blood pressure. The rise in heart rate and pumping action caused by heavy arm exercise increase the heart's oxygen consumption. In addition, expiratory strain against a heavy load while breathholding (Valsalva maneuver) causes abrupt changes in the heart rate and blood pressure which further compromise the functioning of the heart. This condition is magnified when the stomach is full. Cold exposure has two additional effects on the cardiovascular system. The inhalation of cold air may cause reflex narrowing of the coronary arteries and increase cardiac work. Secondly, cold exposure increases blood vessel resistance because of the vessel constriction at the skin to conserve body heat. If a person's coronary circulation is already compromised by atherosclerosis, the effects of arm work in the cold can have serious consequences. "Angina pectoris," or chest pains, and irregular heart rhythms are more common in cold weather than in temperate weather.

Before performing activities such as shoveling snow or cutting wood in the cold, a cardiovascular conditioning program should be established. In addition, attempt to lift light loads only and breathe throughout the movement, i.e., do not strain while breathholding. Do not eat a large meal or drink caffeinated beverages prior to working in the cold. Cigarette smoking can elevate heart rate and increase vasoconstriction of vessels. Thus, the use of tobacco should be avoided before, during, and immediately after working in the cold (or any other time). Individuals with diagnosed heart disease or significant cardiovascular disease risk, should avoid any straining, high intensity arm exercise and especially in cold weather.

Specific Problem Exercises

Several methods of exercise are not necessarily beneficial to the body; some may even be dangerous. Plastic exercise suits prevent the body from cooling itself, and this can be extremely dangerous in warm weather. The increase in sweat rate caused by such suits provides only a temporary water loss and has no effect on long-term, permanent weight control. Use of a sauna may provide a means of relaxation and thus be beneficial under certain conditions. However, the steam sauna should not be used in hot weather or after vigorous exercise. Cooling and rehydration should be the primary goals during recovery.

In ballistic stretching, vigorous bouncing is used to help stretch the muscle. For example, an individual dives at his toes in an attempt to touch them. Ballistic stretching may improve flexibility, but it probably also increases the risk of muscle and joint injury. See Chapter 5 for a detailed explanation.

Figure 3.5 illustrates other forms of exercise which are potentially dangerous. Supine double leg lifts and straight-leg, straight-back sit-ups can create low back problems, especially in individuals with weak abdominal muscles. Both exercises often cause the pelvis to be tilted creating an arched, hyperextended position (swayback). An alternative to supine leg lifts are side leg lifts or knee to chest leg lifts. In these exercises the back is not prone to hyperextension. Likewise, any movement which places the back in a swayed position (e.g., back bends) should be avoided, especially in young children and other populations with weak abdominal muscles. While these exercises may stretch the abdominal region and increase trunk flexibility, they put too much strain on the lower back. Sit-ups can be performed correctly with the knees bent and a curling motion of the

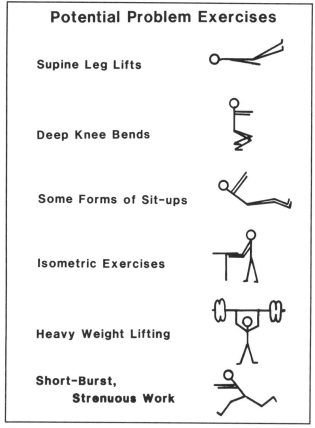

Potential Problem Exercises

Supine Leg Lifts

Deep Knee Bends

Some Forms of Sit-ups

Isometric Exercises

Heavy Weight Lifting

Short-Burst, Strenuous Work

Figure 3.5. *Examples of problem exercises.*

back. In this way, the abdominal muscles are stressed and the end of the up-phase (head between knees) becomes a beneficial lower back stretching exercise. Generally, it is recommended that the feet not be held since this increases the tendency to invert the lower back during the initial stage of the exercise.

Deep knee bends put excess strain on the ligaments of the knee joint. Partial knee bends can be performed or, more appropriately, leg extensions on the weight machine.

Push-ups are excellent exercises for the upper body, but they must be performed correctly. The back must be kept straight and not allowed to sag (Figure 9.61). Individuals who cannot maintain a straight back should perform modified push-ups using the knees instead of the feet for a base.

Isometric and heavy lifting exercises are not necessary for individuals attempting to achieve general physical fitness. Both types of exercise, and especially isometrics, cause the muscle to occlude the arteries in the area, and decrease blood flow to exercising muscles. This increased resistance to flow raises systolic and diastolic blood pressure. In addition, straining while breath-holding (Vaisaiva maneuver) increases chest (intrathoracic) pressure and reduces the amount of blood which can enter the heart's chambers. Thus the heart has less blood available to pump out. The decrease in stroke volume causes a compensatory increase in heart rate to maintain cardiac output. This response is a less efficient mechanism than found in rhythmic activity in which cardiac output is increased by elevations in both stroke volume and heart rate. Although breathing during the activity can help prevent the increase in intrathoracic pressure, the rise in blood pressure is still a potential problem. Lighter weights can be used in weight training, but isometrics are not recommended since even mild exercise can cause a large rise in blood pressure. Heavy weight training requires skill and supervision and generally is contraindicated for untrained individuals over 40 years of age because of the additional adverse effect of atherosclerosis on blood pressure in many of these individuals.

Like isometric exercise, short burst, high intensity exercise is of little benefit in the general fitness program. Such activity is certainly advantageous to someone training for competitive racing, but serves little purpose to someone interested in pursuing general physical fitness. Activities such as tennis or racketball should not be part of the initial exercise program. In these anaerobic activities, the heart is often taxed too much and then made to recover too abruptly for the unfit person. Short burst activities can be reserved for diversity after a reasonable amount of fitness has been obtained. These activities can then serve as supplements and divergencies in a general fitness program. High intensity, anaerobic activities should never constitute the primary type of exercise in the general fitness program.

SUGGESTED READINGS

1. Atha, J. Strengthening muscle. *Exercise and Sport Sciences Reviews*. Vol. 9, D.I. Miller, ed. Franklin Institute Press, 1-74, 1981.
2. Fox, W.L. and D.K. Mathews. *The Physiological Basis of Physical Education and Athletic*. Philadelphia: Saunders College; Chapter 7, 1988.
3. Gettman, L.R. and M.L. Pollock. Circuit weight training: A critical review of its physiological benefits. *The Physician and Sportsmedicine* 9:44-60, January, 1981.
4. Stone, W.J. and W.A. Kroll. *Sports Conditioning and Weight Training Techniques*. Boston: Allyn and Bacon, Chapter 2, 1982.
5. Thomas, T.R. and C.J. Zebas. *Scientific Exercise Training*. Dubuque: Kendall/Hunt, Chapter 9, 1987.

PHYSIOLOGICAL EFFECTS OF RESISTANCE TRAINING

Exposing a muscle to progressive overload affects many components of muscular function. The largest effect probably can be seen within the muscle itself, but other systems, such as the nervous and cardiovascular, also are altered with resistance training.

NERVOUS SYSTEM CHANGES

Research studies and athletes' experiences indicate that improved coordination, speed, and performance often are results of muscular resistance training. Surprisingly not all of these improvements can be attributed to physiological changes within the muscle. The central nervous system and the nerve supply from the brain to muscles (motorneurons) contribute to the enhanced muscular function. The "training" of the nervous system appears to occur in three ways: 1. improved nerve transmission efficiency. 2. turning-off "nervous inhibitions," the built-in safety devices which inhibit maximal muscular efforts. 3. enhanced maximal motor unit recruitment. A great deal of scientific evidence supports the importance of nervous involvement in muscular training. One such phenomenon is called "cross transfer" in which training one limb can cause strength gains in the opposite or contralateral limb. Athletic trainers and physical therapists have used this principle for many years. For example, when an individual has a leg in a cast, exercise training with the healthy leg can offset the loss of strength and size in the injured limb. Thus, the injured limb gets some exercise even though it is casted. What happens in cross transfer is that the muscles of the two legs have some nerves in common. Training these common nerve pathways by single leg exercises, allows some transfer of the nerve effect to the opposite leg.

Measurement of electrical activity to muscle can be performed by electromyography (EMG). The electromyograph simply detects the amount of electrical stimulation from the central nervous system arriving at a given muscle. Placement of electrodes allows the selection for measurement of a specific muscle or group of muscles. Electromyography illustrates that different amounts of stimulation are required for different activities of muscle. For example, in recruiting more motor units to lift the heavier object in Figure 1.3, more EMG activity would be recorded. As the muscle becomes stronger with resistance training, fewer motor units are necessary to move a given load; thus less electrical stimulation to the muscle is required, and less EMG activity would be recorded after training.

Some aspects of muscular function gains involve other means of enhancing nervous pathways from the brain to the muscle. Magnifying stimulation to muscle can be accomplished by removing neuronal inhibitions. Certain "negative" factors are involved in transmitting electrical signals to muscle (Figure 4.1). In effect, these inhibitors "turn-off" muscular contraction. Such mechanisms probably are protective of the muscle. They do not allow it to contract so vigorously that serious injury might occur. But these inhibitions may limit the maximal amount of strength exhibited by a

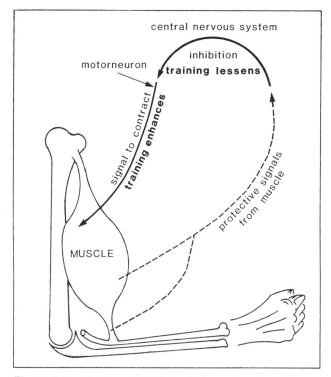

Figure 4.1. *Nervous inhibition of muscular strength performance. A protective inhibition reflex in the tendon prevents the muscle from achieving maximal muscular tension.*

muscle. Through resistance training, these inhibitions are decreased. The stronger muscle, therefore, is less inhibited (Figure 4.1). Because the muscle and surrounding connective tissue are stronger, less neural inhibition is necessary for protection. By improving neural input efficiency, the muscle can exhibit greater strength. This neuronal component of muscular function is one reason why strength and power gains may occur in the absence of muscular hypertrophy or other changes within the muscle. Improved performance with shouting and superhuman feats of strength also may be examples of extra-ordinary neural input and the "turning off" of contracting inhibitions.

Neural training also involves alterations in motor unit recruitment. Although fewer motor units are recruited during submaximal lifts, the trained individual has the ability to recruit additional motor units during maximal efforts. The very largest neurons and fibers are the hardest to stimulate. High intensity resistance training improves the athlete's ability to recruit these larger, stronger motor units.

Improved neural activity probably accounts for most of the improved muscular function which occurs during the early stages (first several weeks) of a resistance training program. After this time, nervous system changes may plateau and muscular alterations account for continued improvement in muscular strength and performance.

MUSCULAR CHANGES

Muscular Hypertrophy

Although neural training is important, the most dramatic alterations caused by resistance training are within the skeletal muscle and associated connective tissue. The most visible change occurs in the size of the muscle. The disruption of the fiber, especially at the z-discs, caused by heavy resistance exercise, dramatically enhances protein rebuilding by the muscle cell nucleus. This muscular hypertrophy is primarily centered at the sarcomere level with increased myosin, actin, and regulatory proteins. The addition of sarcomeres stimulates the formation of new myofibrils, and these changes make the muscle fibers larger.

Enzymes are chemicals within the muscle cell which catalyze or promote biological reactions. During exercise, these are especially important in the production and use of ATP by

Table 4.1. *Factors of Muscular Hypertrophy*
1. sarcomere protein: myosin, actin, regulatory proteins
2. enzymes: anaerobic and aerobic?
3. cellular energy sources: APT-CP, glycogen
4. connective tissue: ligament and tendon size and strength
5. total mitochondria (but mitochondrial "density" decreases)
6. total blood supply (but capillary "density" decreases)

muscle. Enzyme changes following resistance training are somewhat inconsistent. Anaerobic enzymes, such as lactate dehydrogenase, may stay the same or even decrease following heavy resistance training. Aerobic enzymes, such as citrate synthase and succinate dehydrogenase generally decrease. The exception to these findings is found in body building type of resistance training. These lifters generally exhibit aerobic enzyme activity which is higher than untrained and traditional strength trained individuals. Apparently the lower loads and greater sets associated with body building resistance exercise stimulates the oxidative metabolism of slow-twitch fibers to a greater extent than traditional heavy resistance exercise.

Mitochondria, the site of aerobic metabolism in the cell, are more numerous following resistance training. Additional capillaries also are induced and carry increased blood supply to greater muscle tissue. However, the increase in fiber size is generally greater than the increase in mitochondria or capillaries. The "density" of these items, therefore, is reduced. That is, the hypertrophied muscle has lower mitochondria/fiber and capillary/fiber ratios than the untrained muscle.

In addition to protein constituents, enhanced substrate stores of ATP-CP and glycogen occur through supercompensation. Therefore, more quick energy is available for exercise in the trained muscle. All of these changes make the muscle a more efficient contractile machine, stronger, and able to perform more work.

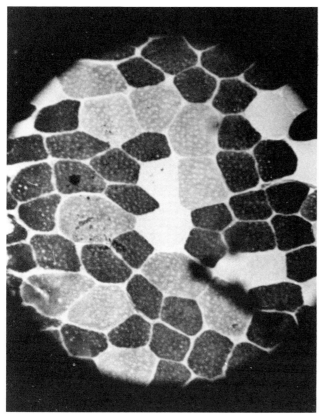

Figure 4.2. Muscle fibers following a heavy resistance training program. The darkest cells are slow twitch, the lightest cells are fast-twitch II a, the gray cells are fast twitch II b. Notice the larger size of the fast twitch fibers.

Both slow twitch and fast twitch muscles increase in size and strength with resistance training. However, in most cases, the FT muscle fibers are used more extensively in resistance exercises, and they develop to a greater extent than ST fibers (Figure 4.2). The Type II a fast twitch fibers may grow the largest. These fast twitch fibers have both anaerobic and aerobic capabilities. It is interesting that the II a fibers sometimes develop more than the II b, which are the most anaerobic fibers in the muscle.

Since the high threshold FT motor units are recruited in resistance training, the lower threshold ST motor units also must be recruited. Therefore, strength and hypertrophy changes also will occur in ST muscle fibers even with heavy resistance, anaerobic training.

Aerobic Training Interference

Although endurance or cardiovascular training is a critical part of any fitness program, aerobic exercise can interfere with the training of muscular hypertrophy and strength. For example, an individual who works strictly on a muscular resistance program will gain more strength than if he/she worked on a combined aerobic plus resistance program. On the other hand, resistance training does not "dilute" the aerobic capacity increases induced by an aerobic training program. For example, an individual will gain similar improvements in aerobic capacity whether he/she follows a strictly aerobic program or a combined aerobic plus resistance fitness program. Since the interference with strength gains is small, this principle is of little consequence to the person interested in general fitness. But to the power athlete, it presents a dilemma. Aerobic training seems to help the athlete in multi-event contests, at the end of a contest, and late in the season. Endurance training thus is important to most athletes. Yet, such training could dilute the anaerobic training component. Therefore, athletes such as sprinters, throwers, volleyball players, etc., must use aerobic training cautiously while participating in an anaerobic sport.

Anaerobic athletes can use a few of these training strategies to decrease the potential dilution effects of endurance training. 1. The long-distance training can be concentrated primarily in the off-season, as much as 3-4 times per week. 2. Even in the off season, distance should be limited to 2-3 miles of faster paced exercise or long interval work. 3. In-season maintenance can consist of long interval work, such as running hard for 90 sec and jogging for 90 sec. In other words, the aerobic training is performed at higher intensities so that the anaerobic system and fiber types also are stimulated.

Connective Tissue

Resistance training causes improvement of structures which are associated with the muscle. Increases in connective tisssue strength and weight occur with resistance training. Regular "load-bearing" exercise enhances the strength of ligaments, which connect two bones together. In addition, muscular hypertrophy is associated with increases in size and strength of the tendon which attaches the muscle to bone. Physical activity also stimulates bone growth and increased calcium content. Weight-bearing exercise usually has a beneficial effect on individuals with osteoporisis and calcium deficiency.

Muscular Hyperplasia

Although most of the muscular adaptation is due to the increase in myofibrillar protein and connective tissue associated with muscle, some increase in size and function may occur by increasing the "number" of fibers or cells in a muscle. This multiplication of cells is called "hyperplasia." While some evidence exists for hyperplasia in animals, the occurrence in humans has not been demonstrated. In interesting experiments at the University of Texas, Dr. William Gonyea has trained cats to lift ~40% of their body weight with one paw for food. This heavy progressive resistance program apparently produced increased fiber number in the trained limb. These results have not been duplicated in humans, and it is still unknown if meaningful hyperplasia occurs in other animal species. However, the possibility cannot be ruled out.

Fiber Interconversion

True fiber type interconversion probably does not occur as a result of resistance training. That is, ST fibers do not convert to FT fibers with anaerobic training. Likewise, FT fibers do not become ST fibers with aerobic training. Such interconversions would require a switch in nerve type as well, since the two main fiber types are innervated by different kinds of neurons. (See Chapter 2.) However, it is possible that the two kinds of FT fibers, IIa and IIb, can interconvert. In heavy resistance training, increases in IIa fibers may occur accompanied by decreases in IIb, suggesting interconversion. In sprint training, increases in IIb fibers have been shown to occur. The increases in FT IIa fibers with weight training give the muscle a greater anaerobic as well as aerobic prowess than in the untrained condition.

CARDIOVASCULAR EFFECTS

During resistance exercises, dramatic adaptations in function can occur in the heart. Intense contraction of muscles causes the obstruction of blood flow to the contracting muscle. This altered "resistance" to blood flow, increases the load against which the heart must pump and therefore increases the force of the heart's contraction (Figure 4.3).

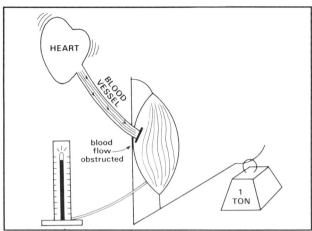

Figure 4.3. *Resistance exercise and blood pressure. Intense muscular contractions increase the resistance for the heart and thus increase blood pressure.*

Blood Pressure

The blood flow obstruction coupled with the force of the heart beat causes an elevation in blood pressure. In addition, large increases in the pressure will occur in the chest cavity surrounding the heart (intrathoracic pressure) if the breath is held during the lift. This Valsalva maneuver further increases the load on the heart. The magnitude of these cardiovascular effects is dependent on the amount of resistance the muscle is attempting to move, the extent of breathholding, the muscle mass involved, and most importantly the nearness to failure. For example, lifting heavy resistance (90% 1RM) to failure with the legs while breathholding would produce the greatest cardiovascular effect. This pressure response increases with each repetition, so that even with lighter loads, the response is near maximal if repetitions are performed to failure.

Average blood pressure of 350/280 mmHg have been measured during double leg presses by experienced body builders. These values compare to resting blood pressure of 120/80 and aerobic exercise blood pressures of about 150/80. Research using middle-aged adults indicated that systolic pressures can reach as high as 230 mmHg and during bench presses using only 50% of maximum. The pressure elevations are slightly less in persons who are experienced with resistance training. The long term effects of the periodic, transient pressure elevations are unknown, but resistance training does not seem to elevate resting blood pressure. That is, normal resting blood pressure is found in most weight lifters if the appropriate cuff size is used to measure the pressure in the enlarged arm. Still, the acute blood pressure response during resistance exercise suggest some guidelines (Table 4.2).

Table 4.2. *Guidelines for Resistance Training Based on Blood Pressure*

1. Resistance training using loads greater than 50% of maximum should not be performed by individuals with known cardiovascular disease or high blood pressure.

2. Resistance training with loads greater than 50% of maximum should not be performed without medical clearance by individuals with cardiovascular disease risk factors such as smoking, obesity, or elevated blood fats.

3. Older individuals (>40 years), whose vessels are less elastic, should not perform resistance exercises using loads greater than 50% of maximum.

4. Persons interested in general muscular fitness should use loads of 40 to 60% of maximum.

5. Persons interested in general muscular fitness should not lift to complete failure.

6. Breathing should be continuous and rhythmic throughout the lifts. The Valsalva maneuver should be avoided.

7. Heavy resistance training using loads greater than 75% of maximum should be reserved for competitive athletes.

8. After their competitive playing days, athletes should decrease the loads of resistance training workouts.

Oxygen Consumption

Traditional weight training exercises produce little effect on maximal oxygen consumption. Although heart rates can be quite high, around 75-85% of maximum, the oxygen cost of even heavy resistance exercise is relatively low, about 45-50% of maximum (Table 4.3). Thus, the aerobic system often is not taxed enough to improve during this type exercise. In comparison, walking uses a similar relative heart rate and oxygen consumption. The comparable relative heart rates and oxygen consumptions in aerobic walking are more beneficial for the cardiovascular system than the dissimilar high intensity heart rates and low intensity oxygen consumption exhibited with heavy resistance training. Recently the development of machines which do not use weight stacks allow the heart rate and oxygen consumption intensities to be better matched. Regardless of the machine, the most appropriate exercise for beneficial cardiovascular effect is circuit resistance training (CRT). In this system, lighter loads of about 40-60% maximum are used with more repetitions, 12-15, than the traditional strength training regimen. In addition, rest periods of only 15 seconds are taken between exercises or sets. In this way, the heart rate remains elevated through the workout, and the relative oxygen consumption is increased. The exercise heart rate and oxygen consumption are more closely coupled at 65 to 70% and 45 to 50%, respectively. The major reasons for using resistance training, i.e., strength and bulk gains, are sacrificed somewhat with CRT, but scientific studies show how significant strength and lean body weight gains are possible with this program. (For a specific CRT program, see Chapter 11.)

Heart Hypertrophy

Increases in the size of the left side of the heart (left ventricle) occur with both endurance and heavy resistance training. Because the two types of exercise provide different overloads for the heart, the left heart hypertrophy is somewhat different. Heavy weight lifting is associated with large increases in vascular occlusion and a high resistance against which the heart must pump (Figure 4.3). This type of exercise is associated with a lower blood output with each heartbeat (reduced stoke volume).

Table 4.3. *Coupling of Heart Rate and Oxygen Consumption in Different Exercises*

Exercise	Heart Rate	% of Maximal Heart Rate	% of Maximal Oxygen Consumption
weight machine and free weights	155-165	75-80	34-40
non-weight resistance machines	145-155	70-75	45-50
circuit weight training	135-145	65-70	45-50
walking	120-130	60-65	50-55
jogging	140-150	70-75	55-60

The physiological response of the heart against this enhanced resistance to flow produces an increase in heart muscle wall thickness. Historically, this enlarged heart was called the "athlete's heart." But the size alone does not make it healthy. The cavity or chamber of the left heart of competitive lifters is normal. Therefore, virtually all of the heart hypertrophy in these individuals is due to the increased musculature; the heart's mass/volume ratio is greater than an untrained person's (Figure 4.4). This type of enlargement is termed concentric or afterload hypertrophy. In contrast, the endurance trained athlete's heart has greater musculature plus a large chamber, thus a normal mass/volume heart ratio. This type of increased size is called eccentric or preload hypertrophy. The increased chamber size is believed to be indicative of a more efficient heart and may allow greater increases in the heart's output during vigorous exercise.

Most of the measurements of the enlarged heart have been made on competitive, heavy weight lifters. Scientific studies performed at the University of Texas, suggest that non-competitive weight lifters have left heart hypertrophy but normal mass-to-volume ratios. These findings suggest that only in very heavy resistance training does heart hypertrophy "over-develop" compared to chamber size. It is unknown how long or how heavy the resistance training must be to produce the "weight lifter hypertrophy" of the left heart. Much of the cardiovascular research suggests that muscular resistance training must be conservative. Lighter resistance (40-60% of maximum) will produce muscular strength and tone and not dilute cardiovascular fitness. In addition, resistance training should be coupled with a consistent aerobic exercise program. By combining these regimens, greater total physiological fitness can be more assured.

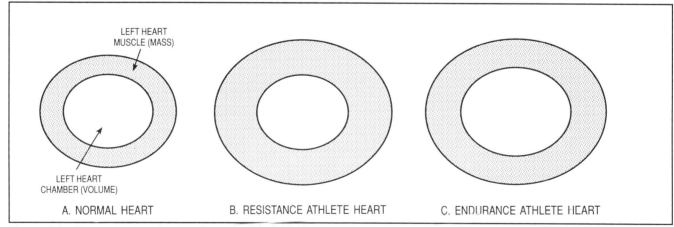

Figure 4.4. *Heart size in trained and untrained individuals. In B, the heart muscle mass increases more than the heart chamber (concentric hypertrophy). In C, the heart muscle mass and heart chamber both increase proportionately (eccentric hypertrophy).*

32

HDL-Cholesterol

The levels of HDL-cholesterol (HDL-C) in blood is an indication of an individual's susceptibility to cardiovascular disease. Low blood levels are associated with greater occurrence of atherosclerosis and reduced blood flow to the heart and brain. Blood HDL-C is much higher than normal in endurance trained athletes. These values can be elevated in previously sedentary individuals who undertake systemic aerobic training for one year.

In general, anaerobic training such as resistance exercise does not affect HDL-C levels. Because many power athletes maintain a high protein, high fat diet, the amount of saturated fat is increased and the total cholesterol in the blood may be elevated. If HDL-C remains unchanged, the cholesterol/HDL-C ratio can be increased in power athletes. That is, the percentage of the total cholesterol carried by HDL is lower than normal. This in itself can indicate greater risk to cardiovascular disease.

Resistance trained athletes who use anabolic steroids have extremely low blood levels of HDL-C, often 50% less than normal. When steroid intake is terminated, the blood lipid profile generally returns to normal. The long-term affect of such low HDL-C values is unknown, but at least temporarily such athletes may be very susceptible to the atherosclerotic process.

SUGGESTED READINGS

1. Lamb, D.R. *Physiology of Exercise: Responses and Adaptations.* New York: MacMillan, Chapters 2 and 13, 1984.
2. Fleck, S.J. and W.J. Kraemer. Resistance training: physiological responses and adaptations (parts 2 and 3). *Physician and Sportsmedicine* 16:108-124, 63-74, April and May, 1988.
3. Vogel, J.A. Symposium: physiological responses and adaptations to resistance exercise. *Medicine and Science in Sports and Exercise* 5 (supplement):S131-S168, 1988.

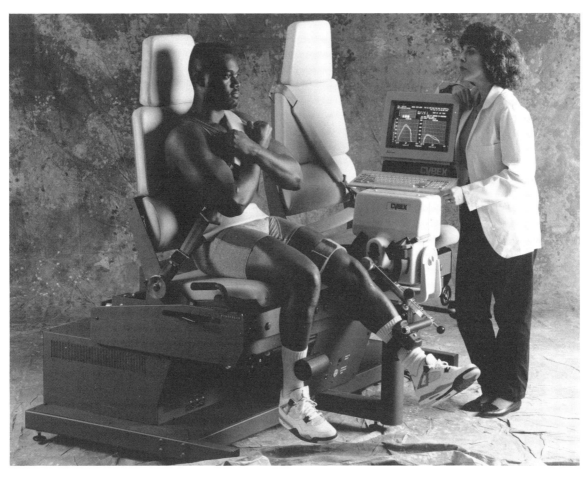

33

16. 1) to prevent tearing injuries to the connective tissue surrounding the muscles and joints.
2) to improve performance by increasing the range of motion about a joint
3) to prevent muscle soreness.
4) promotes a sense of well-being
5) is ~~phys~~ psychologically beneficial because it relaxes the exercise participant.

17. Tendons, muscle sheath, ligaments, and joint capsules.

18. Ballistic stretch — Side stretch exercise, in which one hand is on the hip while the other hand is extended overhead. The upper body p 36 - 37

19. p 49
20. p 50
21. p 53
22. p 57
23. p 61
24 p 62
25. Muscle Glycogen
Adipos Triglycerides (TG)
Liver Glycogen and Blood Glucose
Muscle Tryglycerides

PRE-EXERCISE ACTIVITY: WARM-UP AND STRETCHING

CHAPTER 5

Carole J. Zebas, P.E.D.

INTRODUCTION—WHY WARM UP?

Historically, exercise participants have employed some type of "warmup" before proceeding with an exercise bout. It has been thought, although not proven conclusively, that the benefits of warming up are: (1) to prevent tearing injuries to the connective tissue surrounding the muscles and joints; (2) to improve performance by increasing the range of motion about a joint; and (3) to prevent muscle soreness. It also has been suggested that warming up promotes a sense of well-being, and perhaps, is psychologically beneficial because it relaxes the exercise participant.

The term "warm up" generally is used to describe the pre-activity undertaken before performing an actual exercise bout such as jogging, walking, swimming, or resistance training. However, a controversy exists over just what "warming up" means? Is it the elevation of muscle tissue temperature? Is it stretching the connective tissue surrounding the muscles and joints? Or is it a combination of both of these? To answer these questions, it is necessary to examine more closely the scientific aspects of the interrelationship between muscle and connective tissue.

SCIENTIFIC ASPECTS OF MUSCLE AND CONNECTIVE TISSUE

There are two issues which must be addressed to better understand what warming up is and what benefits result from pre-exercise activity. One is the physiology of muscle temperature elevation, and the other is the biomechanics of connective tissue elongation.

Physiology of Muscle Temperature Elevation

Muscle tissue temperature may be elevated by doing activities such as light jogging,

walking, taking a hot shower, or sitting in a sauna. On the other hand, temperature may be raised by performing the desired activity at a submaximal level. In resistance training, this could mean lifting light weights through a range of motion. It generally is thought that a warmed muscle is less likely to become injured. In other words, it would take a greater force and length of stretch to "tear" the muscle.

Several benefits accrue from the elevation of muscle tissue temperature. Circulation is increased making oxygen more available to the muscle cells. This results in more energy being made available for muscle contraction. The increase in muscle temperature also speeds up the metabolic processes to produce more forceful contractions. Additionally, the elevated temperature reduces muscle stiffness, making the muscle more extensible. This, in turn, makes the muscle contraction smoother. Finally, the elevated muscle tissue temperature helps to relax the muscle and make it perform more efficiently.

Biomechanical Properties of Connective Tissue

Connective tissues are found in and around the muscles. They are the tendons, muscle sheath, ligaments, and joint capsules. These are the structures which can enhance movement or can inhibit it.

These important connective tissues have viscoelastic properties which are responsible for length increases. One of these properties is termed "viscous" and is characterized by the ability to remain permanently deformed once it has been subjected to stretch. This same effect can be seen in pulling taffy. Once the taffy has been stretched, it does not return to its original shape. The second property, which is called "elastic," has just the opposite effect. Once it has been subjected to a stretch, it returns back to its original shape. This is much like the effect of removing a rubber band from around a package. Once it has been removed, it returns to its original shape.

Both viscous and elastic properties are found in connective tissue. The property which acts to a greater degree is dependent upon the type of stretching, the temperature to which it has been subjected, and the rate at which the stretch has been applied. The domination of the viscous property is highly desirable for increased range of motion or extensibility. The stretching exercises which enhance this property are the ones which are of a long, slow stretch variety. This includes the static stretch, partner-assisted passive stretch, and the modified proprioceptive neuromuscular facilitation (PNF) stretch. As the temperature rises, the viscous property dominates. This lends support to the idea that the muscle tissue temperature should be elevated before stretching begins.

STRETCHING EXERCISES

Recent studies on stretching and its relationship to muscle and connective tissue injury have produced some interesting conclusions. Most importantly, there is little evidence to support the idea of pre-stretching before an exercise bout to prevent injuries from occurring. The main reason given for this notion is that most exercise bouts are not rigorous enough to warrant stretching beforehand, and the risk of injury is minimal. However, in contrast, stretching prior to exercise bouts that involve quick movements or movements with large ranges of motion appear to benefit from stretching. Injury risks are reduced and performances are more efficient due to the increases in ranges of motion around the joints.

The decision to stretch or not to stretch becomes easier to make when the issue of muscle tissue warming is included. Much more positive benefits from pre-exercise activities result when the muscle temperature is elevated prior to performing stretching exercises.

Types of Stretching Exercises

There are four commonly accepted types of stretching exercises. They are the ballistic stretch, static stretch, partner-assisted passive stretch, and the modified proprioceptive neuromuscular facilitation (PNF) stretch.

The "ballistic stretch" or fast stretch exercise is characterized by a bouncing movement as a person attempts to move through a range of motion. An example might be the side stretch exercise in which one hand is on the hip

while the other hand is extended overhead. The upper body is moved sideways at the waist toward the hand which is on the hip. When the body can no longer move any farther, it is brought back up to the standing position. The action is repeated several times in succession giving an appearance of a "bouncing" manneuver. The disadvantage of this type of exercise is that the bouncing motion contributes to micro-tears in the connective tissue and muscles of the body. It also has the tendency to cause muscle soreness.

The "static stretch" or slow stretch exercise is characterized by a slow stretch through a range of motion followed by a holding of that position. An example of this exercise might be one for stretching the muscles of the calves. The person performing the exercise leans forward against a solid object (e.g., wall) with the leg which is not being exercised in the forward position (Figure 5.1). The body is lowered forward toward the wall as the extended leg with its knee in a straight position is being stretched. This is a popular stretching exercise because it eliminates the muscle soreness associated with the ballistic type of exercise and avoids the small tears in the muscle caused by the bouncing action.

The "partner-assisted passive stretch" exercise, as it name suggests, involves two people. One person performs the exercise while the second person applies the stretch. It is called a passive exercise because the person performing the exercise is not actively involved in moving through a range of motion. An example might be an exercise designed to stretch the hamstrings (Figure 5.2). The person performing

Figure 5.1. *Example of a static stretch exercise. The continuous stretch on the calf is held for 6 to 30 seconds.*

Figure 5.2. *Example of a partner-assisted stretch exercise. The partner moves the limb through a range of motion. The performer does no active moving of the limb.*

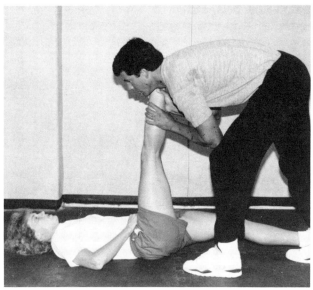

Figure 5.4. *Second phase of PNF exercise. Partner provides resistance as exerciser attempts to move leg back toward the ground, causing an isometric contraction of the hamstrings and gluteals.*

the exercise sits on the floor with the legs spread out. A partner reaches over the out. A partner reaches over the performer's shoulder and grasps one of the legs just above the ankle. The partner than draws the leg up toward the chest of the performer. The performer, in this case, does no active moving of the leg. A potential danger of this exercise is overstretching.

The "modified PNF stretch" is a slow stretch exercise combined with an isometric contraction. It must be performed by two people, one who moves through the range of motion, and

the other who provides the resistance for the isometric contraction. An example might be an exercise in which the hamstrings are stretched. The person performing the exercise is in a back-lying position with both legs extended. One leg is then bent at the waist and brought upward toward the head as far as possible (Figures 5.3, 5.4, 5.5). When the leg has reached the limit of its range of motion, an attempt is made to return it to its original position. However, a partner provides resistance to this motion by prohibiting any forward movement from occurring. This is the

Figure 5.3. *Example of the first phase of a PNF exercise. The leg is elevated and pulled toward the head as far as possible.*

Figure 5.5. *Third phase of PNF exercise. The performer again attempts to move the leg toward the head.*

isometric contraction. After approximately 10 seconds, the resistance is removed and the performer attempts to move the leg in the original motion toward the head. Some exercise specialists encourage the partner to assist in the last stretch, thus making it a passive motion on the part of the performer. Herein lies the disadvantage of this exercise. First, it relies on two people to complete the exercise. Second, the partner providing the resistance and last stretch must be careful to avoid soft-tissue injury to the performer by overstretching.

The modified PNF stretching exercise is called a "modified" technique because it has several variations. The example of the exercise just described is called the "hold-relax" technique. It is probably the most popular technique currently used by athletes and other exercisers. The other variations mainly differ in the group of muscles undergoing the isometric contraction (i.e. the muscle to be stretched or its opposite muscle counterpart). The partner assisted stretching routines might be practical only when partners are training by free weight resistance exercise.

The Stretch Reflex

When a muscle is stretched, a sensory structure within the muscle becomes active. This nerve and muscle complex is the "muscle spindle." It is a modified muscle fiber contained within a capsule and has a sensory nerve spiraled around its center. The muscle spindle is sensitive to any stretch placed on the muscle and serves as a protective device to prevent overstretching. When the muscle is stretched, the muscle spindle and,

more specifically the sensory nerve, is activated. An impulse is sent to the central nervous system which in turn sends impulses by the motor nerves to cause contraction of the muscle fibers. This phenomenon is known as the stretch reflex, and when activated, this relfex inhibits stretching.

The static and modified PNF stretching exercises both contain sustained movements which do not activate the stretch reflex immediately. Thus, the muscle can be stretched further and range of motion can be enhanced. The ballistic stretch exercise, where movements occur rapidly and are repetitive in nature, vigorously activates the stretch reflex, and contraction of the muscle rather than stretching can occur.

Stretch Relaxation

In the earlier discussion of connective tissue biomechanics, the viscoelastic properties were described. The elastic property allows a stretched tissue to return to its original length and shape. However, while the stretch (or load) is being applied, the elastic property reponds to the action by increasing the tension in the connective tissue. At the same time, the viscous property, which allows a stretched tissue to remain deformed once it has been stretched, repsonds to the rate and duration of the stretch (load). The slower rate and the longer duration of the stretch results in reduced tension in the connective tissue and allows for stress relaxation. This is desirable because it allows the performer to increase the range of motion of the stretch. Because of their slow movements over a longer period of time, the static and modified PNF exercises contribute to stress relaxation. Table 5.1 summarizes the protective effect of the three mjor types of stretching exercises mentioned in this chapter.

Retention of Range of Motion

Stretching exercises must be performed on a daily basis for an increase in range of motion (flexibility) to occur. There may be times, however, when stretching may be impossible to do. An injury or an illness may prevent the completion of the daily routine of exercises. How long can flexibility be retained? Scientific studies have shown that some of the original gains in range of motion can be retained from 4-8 weeks after the cessation of an exercise program. The greatest decline in flexibility occurs within two weeks after stopping, and gradual decline continues after that. There is scientific support for

Table 5.1. *Protective Effect of Stretching Exercises*	
Ballistic	greater tension greater reflex action less stress relaxation
Static	less tension less reflex action greater stress relaxation
PNF	less tension less reflex action greater stress relaxation

the superiority of the static stretch and modified PNF stretching exercises over the balllistic stretch exercise in retaining some original flexibility gains even after stopping for several weeks. The hip and trunk retain range of motion more than any other part of the body. This may be explained, in part, by the fact that these areas of the body are moved through wide ranges of motion in daily activities such as walking.

GENERAL CONSIDERATIONS FOR PRE-EXERCISE WARM-UP/ STRETCHING

Design a pre-exercise program to fit your primary resistance exercise goals. If you plan to do power movements, large range of motion activities, or high repetitions in the activity, be sure to include both a general warmup and a stretching program. The following considerations will make your pre-exercise program a safer and more effective one.

1. Elevate muscle tissue temperature by a warmup activity such as jogging, walking briskly, or submaximal resistance lifting.
2. Do stretching exercises after the muscle temperature has been elevated.
3. Wear comfortable and loose fitting clothing.
4. Exercise both sides of the body.
5. Stretch the major muscle groups involved in the resistance exercises.
6. Stretch slowly to the point of discomfort, but not to the point of pain.
7. Concentrate on being relaxed throughout the movement, and continue smooth and rhythmic breathing.
8. Hold each stretch for 10 to 20 seconds.
9. Repeat each stretching exercise 2-4 times before moving on to the next exercise.
10. Avoid stretching areas of the body which are "overflexible".

GENERAL STRETCHING EXERCISES

The group of stretching exercise in Figures 5.6 to 5.16 may be referred to as a general or fundamental exercise program. These are suggested exercises to use before and after the resistance training workout. The exercises can be performed in the order presented. Variations of these exercises and other sport specific exercises may be found in the books listed in the Suggested Readings at the end of this chapter.

Figure 5.6. Quadriceps (front of the thigh). Face and lean against a wall or chair for support. Grasp one leg at the ankle and draw the heel toward the buttocks.

Figure 5.7. Gastrocnemius/soleus or calf (back side of lower leg). Face and lean toward a wall or chair for support. Place one leg forward with knee bent while back leg remains extended. Lean forward and downward at the ankle of the back leg keeping the heel on the ground.

Figure 5.8. Hip adductors or groin (inside of thigh). Support the hands while in a squat position. Extend one leg out to the side of the body while keeping the foot on the floor. Lean sideways toward the opposite foot.

Figure 5.9. *Hip flexors (front part of hip and thigh). In a standing position, step forward with one leg and bend to a 90 degree angle. Extend other leg backward and raise it on the ball of the foot. Lower hips while keeping body straight.*

Figure 5.10. *Hamstrings (back of thigh). Sit on the floor with the legs spread out to the side. Keep knees extended, but relaxed, and lean forward. Attempt to touch the head to the knee.*

Figure 5.11. *Trunk rotators. In a sitting position, extend one leg forward. Bend the opposite leg over the outside of the extended leg, and then place the elbow that is on the same side as the extended leg over the outside of the bent leg. Use the free hand to support the body. Look over the shoulder of the support hand and rotate the trunk.*

Figure 5.12. *Lower back. Lie flat on back with hands around knees. Draw knees and head toward chest.*

Figure 5.13. *Chest and abdominals. Lie down on stomach with legs extended backward. Place the hands under the shoulders and push upper body backward. Arch the back and move the head backward.*

Figure 5.14. *Biceps (front of upper arm). Sit on floor with palms facing backward. Extend arms backward until a stretch is felt.*

Figure 5.15. *Triceps (back of upper arm). Reach back of head with one arm. Push elbow downward with opposite hand.*

Figure 5.16. *Shoulder. Grasp a rolled up towel in front of the body. Move hands over the head and behind the body.*

SUGGESTED READINGS

1. Anderson, B. *Stretching*. Bolinas, California: Shelter Publications, Inc., 1980.
2. Beaulieu, J.E. *Stretching for All Sports*. Pasadena, California: The Athletic Press, 1980.
3. Croce, P. *Stretching for Athletics*. New York, New York: Leisure Press, 1984.
4. Holt, L.E. *Scientific Stretching for Sport*. Halifax, Nova Scotia: Sport Research Limited, 1976.
5. Roundtable Discussion: Flexibility. *National Strength and Conditioning Association Journal* 6(4):10-22, 71-73, 1984.
6. Safran, M.R., et al. The role of warmup in muscular injury prevention. *The American Journal of Sports Medicine* 16(2):123-128, 1988.
7. Safran, M. R., et al. Warm-up and muscular injury prevention: an update. *Sports Medicine* 8(4):239-249, 1989.
8. Sapega, A.A., et. al. Biophysical factors in reange-of-motion exercise. *The Physician and Sportsmedicine* 9(12):57-65, 1981.
9. Taylor, D.C., et al. Viscoelastic properties of muscle-tendon units: the biomechanical effects of stretching. *The American Journal of Sports Medicine* 18(3):300-309, 1990.
10. Thomas, T.R. and C.J. Zebas. *Scientific Exercise Training*. Dubuque, Iowa: Kendall-Hunt Publishers, 1987.
11. Zebas, C.J. and M. Chapman. *Prevention of Sports Injuries: A Biomechanical Approach*. Dubuque, Iowa: Eddie Bowers Publishing Co., 1990.
12. Zebas, C.J. and M.L. Rivera. The retention of flexibility in selected joints after the cessation of a stretching exercise program. In *Current Selected Research in Exercise Physiology* (C.O. Dotson and J.H. Humphrey, Eds.). New York, New York: AMS Press, 1984.

MOTIVATION: KEEPING THE MIND PUMPED FOR RESISTANCE TRAINING

CHAPTER 6

Nancy Dunavant King, M.S.

The fitness boom has engulfed people of all ages. More than ever before, children and adults are becoming physically fit. The fitness activities are as varied as the individuals who participate. But all of these individuals, young and old alike, share one common feature that unites them in their pursuit of physical activity: the desire to become healthier. Through education, people have learned that regular physical activity can result in longer life, decrease in illness, and increase in mental functioning. Resistance training has become the exercise of choice for those individuals who wish to incorporate a holistic approach to physical training. While it is not recommended as a sole method of training, resistance exercise is an excellent complement for aerobic activities such as walking, running, biking, or swimming. When performed in conjunction with these and other aerobic activities, resistance training can result in increased strength, speed, and flexibility, as well as decreased percent body fat.

TYPES OF MOTIVATION

While the majority of this book addresses the physiological and biomechanical aspects of resistance training, this chapter is devoted to another important aspect of resistance training: motivation. Motivation is the "why" of physical fitness. Motivation is defined as "something that moves one to act or to continue to act in a certain behavior" (Meyer, 1982). Motivation also has been called "desire" and has been used to describe those factors which motivate us to begin, continue, and feel successful about an endeavor. One's level of performance is dependent upon learned skills combined with the desire to succeed at that particular activity. With the correct skills and a high degree of motivation, an individual can attain his/her peak performance in virtually any activity. On the other hand, peak performance cannot be achieved if a person has the proper skills without the desire to succeed, or vice versa.

While some people are able to motivate themselves completely, others need help from outside sources. There are two types of motivation: extrinsic and intrinsic. Rewards such as money, grades, clothing, praise, and support from others are examples of extrinsic motivation. Intrinsic motivation means doing an activity because of our desire to become more physically fit, to experience the challenge of learning a new skill, performing for the sheer love of the sport, or to achieve certain goals that we have set at the beginning of the program. While both types of motivation are effective, intrinsic motivation is longer-lasting and provides a greater source of satisfaction for the individual whose desire is rewarded by internal rather than external factors.

There are several reasons why people choose to begin and continue a resistance training program. The pursuit of excellence, the desire to achieve what has never been done before, to experience a sense of accomplishment, all are examples of why we become involved in a program that will make us stronger, faster, and more flexible. Social affiliation is another motivating factor; i.e., an individual experiences a sense of belonging when involved in a resistance training program with others who have similar goals. Stress management or stress reduction is another reason why individuals become involved in resistance training. Resistance training allows for a release of mental and physical tension, as well as a greater sense of self-control. After having started with the desire to become more fit, and enduring the process of sore muscles and blisters, the greatest motivating factor is the desire for success. With success comes satisfaction, self-confidence, and the belief that goals can be achieved.

DEVELOPING A MENTAL PLAN FOR PHYSICAL SUCCESS

Before we embark on a trip into unknown territory, it is wise first to check the map, and then outline the route that will be taken to prevent getting lost or sidetracked along the way. Mapping out the route also enables us to determine our final destination and to determine the quickest, yet most efficient way to get there. Without a map, we lose sight of our final destination and wander aimlessly until we become distracted and forget our purpose at the onset. So it is with physical exercise. A map must be drawn to determine the starting and finishing points as well as the route that will be taken in a resistance training program.

Goal-Setting

Once the purpose of the trip has been defined, the first step is to determine the starting point, i.e., our current fitness level. Several physical assessments are described in this book to determine your current level of overall physical fitness. The second step is to determine the final destination, i.e., the final goal(s) of the program and what you hope to achieve. The third step involves the route which will be taken, or the direction that will be necessary to reach the final destination. These three steps describe the goal-setting process and are crucial to peak performance and success in a resistance training program.

The keys to successful goal-setting are to define goals that are realistic yet challenging, specific to your individual needs, and clearly visible on a daily basis. There are three types of goals: long-term, intermediate, and short-term. Long-term goals should be determined first. Long-term goals are the ultimate dreams, what you hope to achieve when all is said and done. These may be attainable in one month, one year, or in a lifetime. Long-term goals for a resistance training program are those specific goals which you hope to achieve as a result of your training. These goals may include being able to bench press a certain amount of weight, or to complete a circuit in a certain amount of time. A well-written, long-term goal might be, "At the end of my program, I will bench press 150 pounds." A poorly-written, long-term goal would be, "At the end of my program, I will be stronger." Also, intermediate goals must be stated in writing, and provide the individual with a series of confidence-builders along the road to the ultimate long-range goals. Short-range goals are those goals that are achieved on a daily or weekly basis and provide individuals with the constant motivation needed to continue a long-term endeavor.

Writing Goals

Listed below are the most important guidelines to follow when defining and writing your goals:

1. Define long-term, then intermediate, then short-term goals in that order.
2. Set goals that are realistic, yet challenging.
3. Set goals that are performance-specific and measurable.
4. Write all goals down and keep them where they are clearly visible every day, perhaps on the bathroom mirror.
5. Goals are not carved in stone, and can be adjusted based on successes or setbacks throughout the program.
6. Keep a written journal every day that describes your daily goals and workout. Constantly compare the daily log to your intermediate and long-term goals to stay on track.
7. Evaluate and re-evaluate goals on a daily basis: Have I achieved what I set out to achieve today? Why? Why not?

Writing each goal on a 3 x 5 note card and posting them in important places is very helpful as a daily reminder of what you want to achieve. Each card should contain one type of goal. For instance, shown below is an example of a 3 x 5 card that lists the long-term goals of a 20-year old woman who is beginning a weight resistance program:

"These are the 5 long-term goals I will achieve at the end of my resistance training program."

1. I will bench press 60 pounds.
2. I will do 100 pounds on leg press.
3. I will squat 150 pounds.
4. I will do 90 pounds on leg extension.
5. I will do 30 pounds on arm curl.

WORKING THROUGH PLATEAUS

Shortly after starting a resistance training program, tremendous improvements in strength, speed, and flexibility are common. Motivation is high, and long-term goals seem right on target. Workouts are fun, confidence is increased, and the pain is minimal. Goals may even be re-written to become more challenging. After a period of time, these large improvements seem to decrease or disappear. There also may be a cessation of improvement altogether. Discouragement and frustration may occur, and motivation is at an all-time low. The body has reached a plateau, or leveling off of performance. Plateaus are natural occurrences in sport, and are necessary for the body to adapt to the physical and mental stresses that have been placed on it. In order to survive a plateau, or series of plateaus that may occur during a resistance training program, the following suggestions are recommended:

1. "Fatigue makes cowards of us all." (Vince Lombardi) Stay motivated by focusing on the long-term goals. Do not give up, but continue to work through the plateau, and work harder if possible. Eventually the body will respond and improvements in performance will resume.

2. Re-adjust the intermediate and short-term goals, but DO NOT re-adjust the long-term goals. These are your dreams for success. Goals should be adjusted so that they are attainable on a daily and weekly basis. Intermediate and short-term goals provide the necessary motivation needed to maintain a high level of interest.

3. Maintain a sense of detachment from performance and self-concept. The tendency to relate one's self-worth as a person to one's performance in the weight room can happen without realizing it. Avoid irrational thoughts such as, "I lifted poorly today, therefore, I will never improve"; or, "I am not getting stronger, therefore, I am lazy."

4. Mental and physical factors that we have no control over can cause plateaus. Illness, fatigue, boredom, and anxiety can place added stress on the body that will affect performance.

5. Realize that plateaus are normal phenomenon in sport and not necessarily negative. They are the body's way of adapting to the stresses being placed upon it. With time, improvements will continue.

6. Examine the cycles of your resistance training program (Chapter 11). Make sure the muscles have adequate rest between exercise sessions (48 hours) and do not work hard at each session. Use a Heavy-Medium or even Heavy-Light weekly plan for each muscle group (Figure 6.1).

7. Increase carbohydrate intake. Feelings of staleness or overtraining can be caused by low muscle glycogen stores.

If not kept in the proper perspective, plateaus can lead to staleness and/or, eventually

burnout. While plateaus can be considered normal and oftentimes temporary, staleness is a more serious state and a precursor to burnout if not addressed. Staleness is an overall physical and emotional state which occurs when an individual performs a skill correctly, but it does not "feel" right. The causes of staleness are more mental than physical but usually involve both aspects. An individual may repeatedly experience feelings of discomfort when exercising even to the extent that he/she begins to feel anxious about working out. Discomfort can turn into constant worry, and the lack of success over a period of time can result in total burnout (Henschen, 1986). Performance decreases during periods of staleness and overtraining (Figure 6.2).

Periods of poor performance can be remedied if kept in the proper perspective and the individual is aware of the symptoms of staleness and/or burnout. Some of the physiological and psychological signs of staleness and/or burnout may be found in Table 6.1.

Preventing staleness or burnout is half the battle. Once an individual experiences some of the symptoms listed in Table 6.1, it is very difficult to resume a high degree of motivation for the activity. If the early signs of staleness and/or

Figure 6.1. *Do not use a "Heavy" regimen for every workout. A heavy day and light day during the week may be helpful during plateaus.*

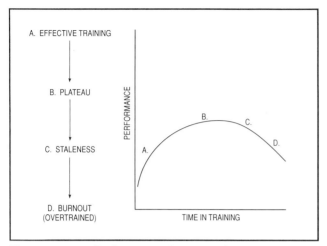

Figure 6.2. *Performance decrement in the overtraining sequence.*

burnout appear, working through the problem may result in injury. If the symptoms are present, total rest or an alternate activity is strongly recommended. Because your desire to perform the activity is very low, it is important to take a break from the activity in which there is no desire and the exercise elicits anxiety and/or worry. This does not mean you need to quit altogether, but rather remove yourself from an activity that is no longer any fun. After a rest, it is common for individuals to return to the training program with more enthusiasm and desire than before he/she experienced the staleness.

INJURIES IN RESISTANCE TRAINING: PSYCHOLOGICAL REHABILITATION

The resistance training program is under way, motivation is high, goals are well-defined, improvement is being made when all of a sudden, an injury occurs. Any number of injuries will cause a setback in the training schedule or cause it to cease altogether for a period of physical and mental healing. With injury comes a feeling of loss: of strength and stamina, of togetherness with those you have been training, of the progress you have made thus far. Preventing additional loss of motivation during the healing period is crucial for a proper mental and physical recovery.

An important element of self-healing during the recovery phase is the visualization of a positive future outcome. By creating mental images of being well and whole, the process of creating a positive future has begun. In creating a mental picture of becoming well again, goal-setting is an important tool for maintaining a positive outlook during a bleak period. If you are not able to exercise at all, a daily routine of mentally practicing your workout can keep you motivated. Because mental images stimulate nerves and muscles, the skill which have been learned will not be totally lost if rehearsed mentally. Mental rehearsal also reinforces desires and long-term goals. Keeping a daily journal of your mental and physical rehabilitation will provide feedback for improvements that would otherwise have gone unnoticed.

GENERAL GUIDELINES FOR STAYING MOTIVATED

Motivation is what moves us to action, and what continues to keep us moving in a certain direction. Peak performance in any endeavor depends on one's skill level and the amount of desire to succeed. Without desire, skill level will not bring success, and without the proper skills, we cannot achieve success on desire alone.

The following guidelines are recommended for achieving success and staying motivated during a resistance training program:

1. Determine WHY you want to participate in a resistance training program. List all the reasons in writing.

Table 6.1. *Symptoms of Staleness and/or Burnout.*	
Physiological	**Psychological**
Higher resting heart rate	Sleep disturbances
Elevated body temperature	Loss of confidence
Weight loss	Quarrelsomeness
Difficulty in breathing	Lack of appetite
Bowel/ digestion disorder	Depression
	Confusion

2. Determine your current state of physical fitness.

3. What would you like to accomplish as a result of being in a resistance training program? List all the long-term goals in writing.

4. Write down the steps or goals you will need to accomplish along the way to achieve your long-term goals. These must be daily, weekly, and monthly goals.

5. Keep a daily journal of what you have accomplished.

6. Re-evaluate goals constantly to make sure you are staying on the correct route.

7. Gain as much knowledge about resistance training as you can by reading and talking to others.

8. Work out with a partner or group for support.

9. Compare weekly progress with your beginning fitness level to build confidence through success.

10. Plateaus are the body's way of adapting to physical and mental stress caused by physical exercise.

11. Rest and diversity are the keys to preventing staleness and burnout.

12. Injured athletes can visualize success and healing during the rehabilitation period to enhance recovery.

SUGGESTED READINGS

1. King, N.J. and D.L. Cook. Helping injured athletes cope and recover. *The First Aider* 56(5): 10-11, March, 1987.

2. Henschen, K.P. Athletic staleness and burnout: Diagnosis, prevention, and treatment. In Williams, J.M. (Ed.), *Applied Sport Psychology: Personal Growth to Peak Performance.* Palo Alto, California: Mayfield Publishing Co., pp. 327-341, 1986.

3. Meyer, P.J. *The Making of a Champion.* Waco, Texas: Athletic Achievement Corporation, 1982.

4. Porter, K. and J. Foster. *The Mental Athlete.* Dubuque: Wm. C. Brown, Publishers, 1986.

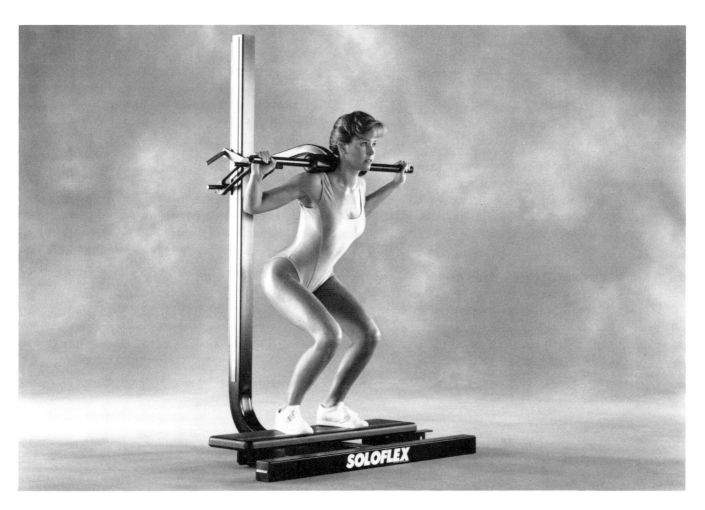

NUTRITIONAL CONSIDERATIONS

Proper intake of nutrients can be a great benefit to the exercising man or woman. On the other hand, dietary excesses are commonplace in Americans and especially in athletes. For the exercising individual a balanced intake of protein and carbohydrate is especially important. In addition, many vitamins and minerals are involved in energy production, and thus adequate intake is vital to exercise performance. Nutritional intake relative to gaining or losing weight will be discussed in the next chapter.

NUTRIENTS

Food intake in the United States has changed dramatically over the past 50 years. One of the most remarkable changes has been the large increase in the intake of simple carbohydrates (CHO) or sugars, especially in soft drinks. The intake of dietary fat also has increased, while the intake of complex CHO such as starch and fiber has greatly decreased. These unhealthy dietary trends seem to be leveling off and even reversing as Americans become more health conscious.

Nutritional deficiencies are rare in the majority of the American population. Rather, nutritional excesses are more common, and supplementing a balanced diet with vitamin and mineral tablets is seldom necessary.

Protein

One of the most important considerations of the resistance trainer is the intake of protein. During heavy resistance training, some of the protein constituents of muscle are broken down. Other protein components, such as certain enzymes, leak out of the muscle cell into the blood during vigorous exercise. These proteins are rebuilt during the recovery period after exercise. (See Chapter 2.) In addition, the process of increasing the synthesis of protein to add muscle bulk and tone requires additional dietary protein.

The primary functions of dietary protein relate to this growth and repair of muscle tissue. Additional functions include the synthesis of hormones, antibodies which fight disease, and enzymes which power metabolic reactions. Very little protein is used as an energy source during exercise, except after prolonged fasting or during very long or repeated exercise when the carbohydrate stores become exhausted.

Protein is essential in the diet of all people in the form of amino acids. The eight essential amino acids (EAA) for the adult are listed in Table 7.1. Only egg, milk, meats, and fish contain adequate quantities of all eight EAA (Table 7.2). These foods are called "complete proteins." Some vegetable products, such as soybeans and cornmeal, contain most of the EAA but have limited amounts of one or two EAA and thus are "incomplete proteins." All EAA must be eaten simultaneously, or perhaps a few hours apart, in order for the body to make the appropriate biological proteins, If an amino acid is lacking, some protein manufacturing may be inhibited. This can be a problem for individuals on a strict vegetarian diet. However, by eating appropriate combinations of plant foods, such as rice and soybeans, all EAA can be obtained from a vegetarian meal.

Table 7.1. *Amino Acids in Foods*	
ESSENTIAL IN ADULTS	
Methionine	Valine
Threonine	Lysine
Leucine	Phenylalanine
Isoleucine	Tryptophan
NON-ESSENTIAL	
Alanine	Histidine (essential
Aspartic Acid	for children)
Arginine	Hydroxyglutamic Acid
Citrulline	Hydroxyproline
Cystine	Norleucine
Glutamic Acid	Proline
Glycine	Serine
	Tyrosine

Table 7.2.	Food Sources for Protein, Carbohydrate, and Fat
NUTRIENT	**FOOD SOURCES**
Protein (essential amino-acids acids)	eggs, meat milk products, fish, legumes, grains
Carbohydrate	grains, pastries, fruits, bread, potatoes, sugar
Fat (linoleic acid)	vegetable oils, margarines, salad dressings, nuts

The recommended dietary allowances (RDA) for protein in the young man and woman are about 56 and 44 g/day, respectively, i.e., 0.8 g/kg body weight. This is only about 2 oz/day and is easily achievable by individuals eating animal foods. The protein requirement is increased only a small amount for individuals involved in moderate intensity exercise programs, such as routine jogging or circuit resistance training. However, in many athletes, and especially those engaged in heavy resistance training and long distance training, the protein need is much greater than normal, about 2-3 g/kg/day. This is equivalent to about 150 g/day or 5.4 oz/day in a man (depending on exercise intensity and body weight) and 120 g/day or 4.2 oz/day in a woman. This amount of protein is more difficult to ingest, but it can be met with the large additional caloric intake found in the athlete's diet. Protein intake for weight gain and weight loss is discussed in the next chapter.

Carbohydrate

Carbohydrate is needed by the body for energy. However, protein can be converted to carbohydrate in the body, and thus this food generally is not considered an essential nutrient. Glycogen and glucose can provide energy very quickly for physical activity. In foods, carbohydrate is eaten as simple sugars, such as sucrose and glucose, or as more complex sugars called starches (Table 7.2.). Most of the complex starch is quickly digested to simple sugars in the intestines. Thus, the blood carries dietary starches and sugars as glucose. Carbohydrate is stored in muscle as glycogen. Some complex carbohydrates, such as cellulose, are not easily digested. Foods such as whole grains, nuts, and other plant products contain roughage or "fiber". This carbohydrate has little value as energy sources but does help digestion of food in the gastrointestinal (GI) track and increases the removal of cholesterol (Table 7.3).

Foods containing a high percentage of carbohydrate can be very diverse in their nutritive value. An orange and candy bar, for example, are both very high in simple sugars. However, the candy bar offers few other nutrients (unless it contains nuts). This food is said to have "empty calories." An orange, on the other hand, is relatively high in carbohydrate calories, but it also contains fiber, calcium, potassium, vitamins A and C, and other nutrients.

Because of the importance of carbohydrate as an energy source during exercise, this food deserves special attention in the diet of the

Table 7.3.	Food Sources for Dietary Fiber	
Total Dietary Fiber		**Cellulose**
whole grain cereals		**and**
whole grain breads		**Hemicellulose**
fruits		bran cereals
vegetables		shredded wheat
nuts		Wheat Chex
		wheat flakes
Pectin		whole wheat bread
soybeans		Grape Nuts
brussel sprouts		Cheerios
carrots		
avocados		**Lignin**
peanuts		bran cereals
walnuts		shredded wheat
grapefruits		Wheat Chex
lemons		wheat flakes
oranges		oat cereal
strawberries		eggplant
		peppers
Methylated Pectin		green beans
apples		
plumbs		
peaches		

Reprinted with permission form T.R. Thomas and C.J. Zebas. *Scientific Exercise Training.* Copyright © 1987 by Kendall/Hunt Publishing Co.

Table 7.4. *Carbohydrate Intake and Exercise*

Time Period	Carbohydrate Intake
24-72 hours prior to exercise	high intake of starches
4-12 hours prior to exercise	normal meal with moderate intake of starches and simple sugars
2-4 hours prior to exercise	light intake of starches or simple sugars
0-1 hour prior to exercise	no carbohydrate intake except fructose
during exercise	light intake of simple sugars, especially liquid
after exercise	high intake of starches

exerciser. During resistance training or athletic competition, it is important to ensure that adequate amounts of glycogen are stored in the active muscles and the liver. Generally this is accomplished by eating meals with complex carbohydrates, such as pasta, breads, and potatoes. Starches eaten 24-72 hours prior to exercise will serve as important energy sources during the exercise (Table 7.4). If exercise is mild during this period, glycogen stores will be greater since it will not be used up as energy (Figure 7.1). Glycogen stores can be increased especially when complex carbohydrates are eaten after vigorous exercise which depletes muscle glycogen.

In general, ample glycogen stores can be maintained in the working muscles simply by routinely including complex carbohydrates in meals. If heavy lifting or competition is maintained over several days, or when prolonged aerobic training is coupled with the resistance training, special carbohydrate loading diets may be necessary. Obviously, too much carbohydrate in the diet can lead to overweight.

A major meal should *not* be eaten within 4-5 hours of resistance training. A light carbohydrate meal, such as juice, toast and jelly, and cookies or a liquid meal, can be taken 2-4 hours prior to the resistance exercise. The energy from this meal generally will not serve as an important energy source during the lifting period. Rather, this food should serve to make the exerciser comfortable and prevent hunger feelings during the exercise.

Immediately prior to exercise, carbohydrate intake can have serious consequences. Sugar intake stimulates the secretion of insulin which causes blood glucose to be taken up by tissues. Exercise also stimulates the uptake of glucose from the blood. The insulin plus exercise response may cause blood sugar to become low, a condition called "hypoglycemia." Since the brain relies heavily on blood glucose as an energy source, dizziness and disorientation can result from hypoglycemia. These observations suggest that carbohydrate should not be eaten within one hour of a contest or exercise bout. Since fructose does not cause such a large insulin response, this carbohydrate can be eaten in small quantities prior to exercise. Commercial solutions of fructose are available.

During exercise small amounts of carbohydrate may be eaten since the exercise will inhibit the insulin response. Food taken during resistance exercise or other activities will not serve as an important energy source for muscle, but can

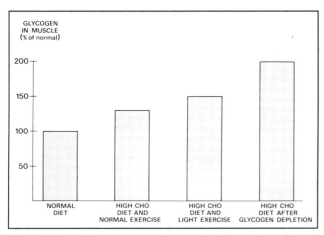

Figure 7.1. *Glycogen stores in muscle after various diet and exercise regimens.*

help maintain blood glucose levels which may benefit the brain.

Following activity, increased carbohydrate intake is necessary to replenish glycogen stores used during the activity. Glycogen synthesis in muscle is especially high during the initial two hours following vigorous exercise. Therefore, carbohydrate intake during this immediate recovery period may be very advantageous for future exercise bouts.

Fats

A major function of fat is to store energy. Stored fats provide about 30-40 times more potential energy than carbohydrate stores. However, fat fuel takes a little longer time to become usable. Fats also serve as building elements of steroid hormones, for example testosterone and progesterone, as carriers of fat soluble vitamins, and as structural components of cell membranes, especially in nerves. Fat is a vital compound, and thus the body synthesizes fats from both carbohydrate and protein sources. Only linoleic acid (an unsaturated fat) is an essential fatty acid since the body does not synthesize this fat.

Cholesterol is an important fat-like substance since it serves as a precursor for the production of the steroid hormones including the sex hormones. But cholesterol is also a component of atherosclerotic plaque and thus may be dangerous when eaten in large quantities. Foods which contain cholesterol are listed in Table 7.5 The American Heart Association suggests reducing the total amount of cholesterol to less than 300 mg/day. This would reduce the number of eggs eaten in any form to no more than seven per week. Some heart disease researchers suggest that even this intake may still be too high, and egg intake may need to be reduced to three per week. Many resistance trainers use eggs to obtain large amounts of essential amino acid. Excessive egg intake should be avoided; seven eggs per week would be a reasonable upper limit for the resistance trainer or athlete.

Two other kinds of fats are important dietary considerations because of their relationship to blood cholesterol. Saturated fatty acids (SFA) found primarily in animal products decrease the excretion of cholesterol which may increase cholesterol in arteries. Unsaturated fatty acids (UFA) are found in vegetable products and help to increase the excretion of cholesterol by the liver. Therefore, these fats are less dangerous than SFA. Some fatty acids are polyunsaturated fatty acids (PUFA), and these are the least dangerous of the fatty acids. Both UFA and SFA are stored in tissue and transported in the blood as part of a triglyceride molecule (glycerol + three fatty acids). During exercise, the trigylceride releases the fatty acids to muscle where both SFA and UFA are used as energy.

Table 7.6 illustrates the relative fatty acid content of some foods. Several nutrition and health organizations have suggested the substitution of UFA foods for SFA foods in the diet. For example, poultry and fish can be substituted for beef and pork at some meals to decrease the amount of SFA in the diet. In addition, skim or half percent milk can be subsituted for whole milk to decrease the amount of dietary fat. Skim milk contains 1 g of fat per cup, 2% milk 5 g/cup and whole milk 8 g/cup. All have about the same amount of protein (8 g/cup), CHO (11g/cup), and vitamins and minerals.

Table 7.5. *Foods and Cholesterol*	
Food	**Cholesterol (mg)**
Liver, chicken (4 oz)	650
Liver, beef (4 oz)	400
Egg (1)	250
Shrimp (4 oz)	160
Lobster (4 oz)	100
Oyster (4 oz)	100
Beef (4 oz)	100
Pork (4 oz.)	100
Lamb (4 oz)	100
Poultry (4 oz)	100
Fish (4 oz)	80
Sausage (1 link)	25
French Toast (2 slices)	260
Cheese (4 oz)	100
Ice Cream (1 cup)	75
Milk, whole (1 cup)	30
Cream Cheese (1 tbsp)	25
Sausage (1 link)	25
Cake (1 piece)	25
Milk, 1% fat	22
Pie (1 piece)	15
Butter (1 tsp)	12
Milk, skim (1 cup)	7
Margarine (1 tsp)	0
Vegetable Oil (1 tsp)	0

Reprinted with permission from I.R. Thomas and C.J. Zebas. *Scientific Exercise Training.* Copyright © 1987 by Kendall/Hunt Publishing Co.

Generally, the major problem for the resistance trainer is taking in too much fat. Because fat is associated with sources of animal protein (e.g., meat, egg, milk), extra fat is eaten by indiviuals seeking to increase protein intake. This association needs to be considered by the exerciser, and the amount of protein and fat intake limited to some degree.

Water Replenishment

Very often resistance training causes the loss of substantial amounts of water and minerals from the body. This is especially true during heavy exercise in a hot or humid room. The degree of sweating can offer some guidelines as to the degree of water replenishment necessary.

Most research indicates that mineral supplements such as salt or magnesium tablets are not necessary following exercise in the heat. While salt especially is lost in sweat, the normal diet usually provides adequate salt to replenish that which was lost. The amount of water lost in sweat is much greater than the minerals.

The extent of water loss or "dehydration" is related to environmental temperature and humidity, core temperature, and exercise duration. Regardless, the replacement of water is the single most important factor for successful exercise in the heat. Cold water or diluted sugar solution (12-18 oz) should be taken 15 to 30 minutes prior to exercise. Small amounts of cold water or solution (4-6 oz) then should be taken frequently, every 15-20 minutes, during the exercise. Even when lifting in a comfortable temperature, the resistance exerciser should drink periodically during the rest periods between stations. Fluid intake should be continued for several hours during recovery. Since the thirst drive lags behind the loss of water, more fluid should be imbibed than feels necessary.

Several factors determine the amount of water that empties from the stomach into the small intestine for absorption. The most important of these factors is the amount of sugar in the fluid. High concentrations of carbohydrate in the form of simple sugars prevent stomach emptying of water. Only fairly dilute sugar solutions should be used (less than 5 g/100 ml (5%) fluid or 20g/12 oz fluid). Glucose polymers (simple sugars bonded together) apparently allow greater amounts of water to be emptied from the stomach than do free simple sugars. Therefore solutions with glucose polymers (e.g., polycose) can have higher concentrations, up to 8 g/100 ml. This concentration allows adequate rehydration as well as

Table 7.6.	*Food Fats Based on Degree of Saturation in the Fatty Acids*

Most Saturated

Coconut Oil
Butter
Mutton
Beef
Pork
Other Red Meats
Poultry
Egg Yolk
Whole Mile
Fish
Olive Oil
Shortening
Margarine
Peanut Oil
Cottonseed Oil
Soybean Oil
Corn Oil
Safflower Oil

Most Unsaturated

Reprinted with permission from T.R. Thomas and C.J. Zebas. *Scientific Exercise Training.* Copyright © 1987 by Kendall/Hunt Publishing Co.

provides a potential energy source through increased blood glucose. Many popular sport drinks have simple carbohydrate or polymer concentrations in the appropriate range. Others are too concentrated for rapid fluid replenishment and should be used only in cool environments or first be diluted with cold water.

The effect of solutions sweetened with saccharin or aspartame is unknown. However, these sweetners probably inhibit water emptying to some degree. Cooler fluids are emptied more rapidly from the stomach than warmer ones. Thus, cool or cold water is probably the most appropriate drink for fluid replacement during and following exercise in the heat. Solutions, such as soft drinks, with large amounts of carbohydrate (~11 g/100 ml fluid or 40 g/12 oz) will not allow adequate water emptying. Likewise, solutions used to replace water loss should have little or no minerals (less than 10 mEq sodium and 5 mEq potassium per liter of solution). Because more water is lost than solids in sweat, the body's mineral concentration is actually increased after exercise. Thus, adding additional minerals will not help the dehydration until the water is replenished. It is wise to read the label for carbohydrate and mineral (electrolyte) content of the popular exercise drinks.

Vitamins and Minerals

Table .8 lists the primary food sources for the major vitamins and minerals. With heavy exercise, some vitamins and minerals are lost from the muscle to the blood and from the blood to sweat. Exercise training increases the need for most vitamins and minerals as well as carbohydrate, fat, and protein, However, the enhanced requirements seem to be easily met with a balanced diet. Even the relatively large amounts of sodium which are lost in profuse sweating can usually be replaced by lightly salting foods. B vitamins, magnesium, and iron play vital roles as cofactors in many of the energy producing pathways. Although exercise increases the requirement of these nutrients, seldom is a deficiency observed even in athletes in intense training. The possible exception to this is iron. Stores of iron have been found to be low, especially in some female athletes. Therefore, active females with normal menstrual cycles may need iron supplementation. Blood tests for hemoglobin, hematocrit, and iron stores can indicate if such supplementation is necessary. (See Chapter 9.)

BODY COMPOSITION

The composition of the human body can be divided into two components: lean tissue (muscle and bone) and fat. Many researchers and physicians believe that body fat amounts are a better indicator of an individual's health status that is total body weight. Overfatness or obesity places more strain on the heart and is associated with hypertension and heart disease. Diabetes also occurs more frequently and is more difficult to control in overweight individuals.

Overweight Children

Obesity in the adult often has its origins at a very early age. Fat cells or "adipocytes" are developed during three stages of life: the last three months of fetal growth, the initial year of life, and at puberty. After puberty the number of fat cells is set and only adipocyte size can be altered. Studies on animals indicate that diet or activity during the periods of fat cell proliferation can effect the eventual number of adipocytes. Thus, even the lifestyle habits of the pregnant mother can affect the eventual number of fat cells in the offspring. Dietary practices in the child also can affect fat cell production. Low fat and moderate caloric intake during childhood and early adolescence may be important to the control of body weight in adulthood. Fat adults invariably have more fat cells than lean adults. When obese adults lose weight, only fat cell size is reduced, and fat cell number is unchanged. Animal studies strongly suggest that exercise during early stages of life can reduce the number of fat cells which are produced. Exercise and dietary practices after adolescence only effect the size of the fat cells and not the number.

The cause of overweight is controversial. Both inactivity and greater caloric intake are probably involved. Regardless, the underlying problem appears to be an increase in the number and size of adipocytes. It is possible that more and larger fat cells alter the appetite "set point" so that more food is eaten to fill these fat cells.

Percent Body Fat Evaluation

What is the optimal or ideal amount of body fat? This question presently is unanswered by scientific information. Because fat is very vital to many body functions, a minimal or essential amount does exist. Some experts have placed this amount at 4% fat (Table 7.8). Females with normal menstrual cycles have an additional amount of *sex specific* fat created by estrogen and progesterone effects. Therefore, the minimal female value is around 9% fat.

Elite endurance trained athletes have % fat values which approach minimum, and they are apparently very healthy individuals. Healthy, active young adults have body fat values well above minimum, about 12% in the male and 22% in the female at age 20. As men and women age, % fat increases due to changes in lifestyle and the naturally occurring decrease in lean body tissue that occurs with aging. For example, the average for a 32 year old active man and woman is about 16% and 26%, respectively. Overfat is generally considered to be 5-10% fat above the age group average. Values for ideal % fat, techniques for calculating % fat and estimating optimal weight are covered in appendix D.

Numerous methods for estimating % fat have been developed, but the most popular methods utilize "anthropometrics," in which body measurements are taken, and "hydrostatic weighing" (HW), in which the individual is weighed while completely submerged in water (Figures 7.2 and 7.3). Both techniques are very

Table 7.7. *Food Sources for Vitamins and Minerals*

VITAMIN	FOOD SOURCES
Fat Soluble	
Vitamin A (retinol)	liver, animal products, green vegetables, carrots, sweet potatoes, fish liver oils
Vitamin D (cholecalciferol)	milk, fish liver oils, eggs
Vitamin E (alpha tocopherol)	vegetable oils, salmon, seeds, whole grains, margarine
Vitamin K (phylloquinone)	intestinal bacteria, green vegetables, whole grains
Water Soluble	
B vitamins	
Thiamin (B_1)	whole grains, nuts, pork
Riboflavin (B_2)	liver, milk, dairy products
Niacin (nicotinic acid)	meats, whole grains, legumes, peanuts
Pyridoxine (B_6)	meats, whole grains, bananas, eggs
Folicin (folic acid)	beans, green vegetables (spinach), whole wheat, liver
Cyancobalamin (B_{12})	meat and animal products (not present in plants)
Panthothenic Acid	liver, meats, eggs, whole grains
Biotin	peas, beans, meats
Choline	egg yolk, liver, grains
Vitamin C (ascorbic acid)	citrus fruits, tomatoes, green peppers, brussel sprouts
Mineral	
Calcium (Ca)	milk, cheese, green vegetables
Phosphorus (P)	milk, lean meats, cheese, grains
Magnesium (Mg)	whole grains, nuts, milk, green vegetables
Potassium (K)	whole grains, meats, fruits potatoes
Sodium (Na)	salt, milk, meat
Chlorine (Cl)	salt
Iodine (I)	iodized salt, sea food, milk
Iron (Fe)	liver, meats, dried apricots, beans, wines, oysters
Copper (Cu)	liver, meat, drinking water
Fluorine (Fl)	water, seafood
Sulfur (S)	meats, eggs, cheese, milk, (sulfur amino acids)
Chromium (Cr)	meats, yeast, vegetable oils
Cobalt (Co)	animal products—vit. B_{12}
Selenium (Se)	meats, seafood, whole grains
Molybdenum (Mo)	organ meats, whole grains, legumes
Zinc (Zn)	liver, meats, seafood, whole grains, cocoa
Manganese (Mn)	whole grains, soybeans, tea, coffee, bananas

Table 7.8.	Percent Body Fat*	
POPULATION	Male AGE 20	Female AGE 20
Minimum	4	9
Endurance Trained	4-8	8-15
Healthy, Untrained (Range)	12 10-16	22 20-26
	Add 1% per 3 years of Aging	
Overfat	20	30

*Values are the amount of fat as a percent of the total body weight. Reprinted with permission from T.R. Thomas and C.J. Zebas. *Scientific Exercise Training.* Copyright © 1987 by Kendall/Hunt Publishing Co.

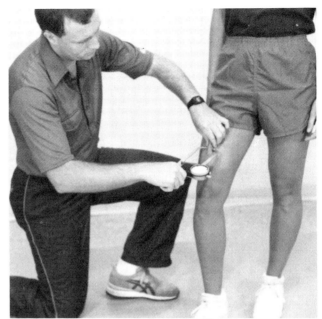

Figure 7.2. *Skinfold measurement. The accuracy of anthropometric estimations of body compositions depend on the skill of the tester.*

useful and both have some disadvantages. The accuracy of anthropometrics depends on the skill of the tester in using the tools, e.g., the skinfold caliper, circumference tape, and anthropometer. Skill is also required in locating the precise anatomical site of the measurement. A third limiting factor is the accuracy of the land weight scale used; some scales may be sensitive only to ± 3 lbs. In the hands of a skilled tester, most anthropometric techniques used on the appropriate population will estimate within 2-3% of the actual % fat. Thus, if an individual is assessed at 15% fat, this might be very close or at least the actual value should be in a range between 12-18% fat. This example illustrates the inappropriateness of using anthropometric values to prescribe body weight loss for individuals who are in the normal or low % fat range. (See Appendix D for skinfold % fat method.)

Hydrostatic weighing, on the other hand, usually can give a very accurate account of % fat. The limitations of this technique include the skill of the tester and the ability of the instrumentation to assess the amount of air in the lungs which, like fat, buoys-up the individual whem submerged. If the air in the lungs is only estimated or crudely measured, then hydrostatic weighing is no more accurate than anthropometrics. The technique is reasonably accurate if this extraneous air is assessed prior to or after the underwater weighing. In the most accurate HW procedure, the lung volume is assessed underwater and at the same time as the underwater weighing. HW with lung volume assessed is accurate and repeatable

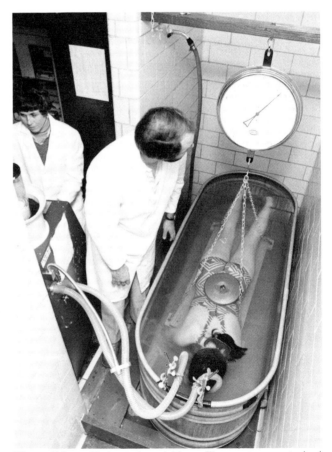

Figure 7.3. *Hydrostatic weighing. The most accurate body composition analysis requires the air in the lungs to be assessed while the subject is underwater.*

within about ±1% fat. Thus, the individual measured at 15% fat is likely between 14-16% fat.

Even the best hydrostatic weighing techniques are biased because of the types of individuals used in early cadaver studies which provide the basis for HW % fat calculations. Data from early research suggest that HW % fat is most accurate within normal ranges, that is, 5-35% fat. For individuals which are extremely lean or fat, any % fat calculation is probably a very crude estimate. Furthermore, the HW procedures are probably more accurate for assessing the % fat of Caucasians than for Blacks and other races.

ERGOGENIC AIDS

A variety of substances have been used to enhance exercise performance. Weight lifting is a sport which traditionally has been associated with the use of ergogenic aids. Generally research studies have not supported the use of performance aids. Most substances do not affect performance in physiological aspect. However, some do have potent psychological effect.

Anabolic Steroids

Probably no other substances have been more controversial in the field of athletics than steroids. Anabolic steroids are synthetic compounds which mimic the effects of testosterone, the male sex hormone. These effects include increased protein synthesis (anabolic) and enhanced male sexual characteristics. Scientific research on the effects of steroid intake on strength and bulk associated with resistance training has not produced consistent results. In general, scientists have found that large doses of anabolic steroids can enhance the strength and lean tissue weight gain produced by a heavy resistance program. Because of this research and testimony by steroids users, many power athletes and competitive lifters are tempted to use these drugs.

It is difficult to deny the potential effectiveness of anabolic steroids in increasing muscular strength and bulk. In only a few athletic events is the need for absolute size and strength critical. More often power and skill are the most important elements of success in a sport. It is doubtful that anabolic steroids help in improving these factors. More importantly, the adverse physiological effects can be dramatic. Most of the detriment caused by steroid use have been observed in patients receiving therapeutic doses for diseases.

However, it is likely that athletes who use steroids can expect similar adverse reactions. These include liver tumors, and cysts, increased secretion of insulin, and alterations in heart muscle and mitochondria. HDL-cholesterol is very low in users of anabolic steroids which indicate an increased susceptibility to cardiovascular disease. In addition, male reproductive function is altered, including reduced sperm production, decreased testicular size, and decreased testosterone production. These drugs potentially have a greater anabolic effect in women, but serious change in the menstrual cycle and reproductive function can occur from steroid use. These alterations apparently are reversible and most reproductive functions in men and women return to normal after cessation of steroid use. However, some residual adverse effects have been observed in normal men after cessation of steroid treatment.

Mood changes and aggressive behavior have been noted in male steroid users. These effects may seem beneficial in certain contact sports, but the athlete may become unable to control the aggression and hostility during the contest or in daily life.

Steroid use is banned by the International Olympic Committee, and other professional organizations have taken firm stands against the use of steroids. Many years of intense scientific study have proven that the serious risks are not worth the potential benefits.

Growth Hormone

Like anabolic steroids, growth hormone enhances protein synthesis in muscle. This hormone from the pituitary also stimulates the growth of connective tissue and bone through the action of hormone-like substances called somatomedins which are produced in the liver. Previously, this hormone has been difficult to obtain because animal growth hormone was not effective in humans, and growth hormone extracted from cadavers was very expensive. However, recent advances in DNA research has allowed the manufacture of synthetic human growth hormone (Protropin). Scientific studies on growth hormone use in athletes are sparse. However, many case studies and personal claims attest to the increased muscle size and strength caused by growth hormone use.

As with anabolic steroids, the potential adverse effects probably outweigh the potential benefits of growth hormone use. Growth hormone increases fat mobilization and may cause fat metabolism disorders (ketosis). It may also increase myocardial wall thickness and stimulate the oxygen consumption of the heart. Symptoms of acromegaly also are common with growth hormone administration. This disorder is characterized by enlarged bones of the head and hands, osteoporosis and arthritis, glucose intolerance, and cardiovascular disease.

Sodium Bicarbonate

"Soda loading" has the potential to improve performance in activities, such as resistance training, which rely heavily on anaerobic energy production. Ingestion of 0.3 g/kg body weight (about 5 teaspoons) about 60 min prior to exercise elevates the amount of bicarbonate in blood. This compound buffers the lactic acid produced during the exercise and stimulates LA removal from the working muscle. In this way, muscle acidity (pH) stays more normal and fatigue may be delayed.

Results from research studies on soda loading have been inconsistent, but several studies have shown improved anaerobic performance and lower ratings of perceived exertion after bicarbonate ingestion. The benefits may be greatest during repeated bouts of vigorous activity when large amounts of lactic acid are produced. However, several intestinal side effects of baking soda ingestion have been reported including stomach upset and "explosive diarrhea."

Phosphate Salts

Phosphate salts have been used as ergogenic aids for over 50 years. It is reported that German soldiers used these tablets in World War I to relieve fatigue. Phosphates may affect exercise performance by: 1. increasing the synthesis of ATP and CP, phosphorous containing compounds which are critical as anaerobic energy sources. 2. increasing 2,3-DPG (2,3-diphosphoglycerate) which enhances the uptake of oxygen from hemoglobin by muscle. Because of the latter mechanism, phosphate salts could enhance performance in aerobic events. These salts may be beneficial in anaerobic events by increasing the pre-exercise stores of ATP and CP. Thus the muscle could rely more on these energy stores and less on anaerobic glycolysis which produces lactic acid.

The dose taken is around 1 g of sodium phosphate four times per day for several days prior to competition or a rigorous training session. No serious side effects have been reported, but the potential benefit for resistance exercise is questionable.

Caffeine

The use of caffeine as an ergogenic aid has been studied primarily in distance athletes. Caffeine is known to stimulate fat mobilization and utilization and thus may spare muscle glycogen in prolonged exercise. In addition, the stimulatory effect of caffeine may increase alertness and neuronal function during exercise. Research examining caffeine and exercise performance is somewhat divided. Caffeine usually increases fat availability but may or may not improve endurance performance. Individuals who do not normally ingest caffeine seem to be more likely to be affected beneficially. That is, when non-coffee drinkers use high doses (750 mg: 7-8 cups of coffee), one hour prior to exercise, improvement in performance is more likely to occur. In these individuals, even performance in brief exercise periods (7-10 minutes) may be enhanced. It is unlikely that caffeine intake will help resistance trainers who use caffeine in the diet.

Vitamins and Minerals

A number of vitamins, including B complex, C, and E have been used in attempts to enhance exercise performance. The majority of scientific research has not supported the use of vitamin supplementation. A possible exception to this is Vitamin C supplementation during exercise in hot environments. Doses of 250 to 500 mg of vitamin C may help the body adapt to a hot environment. Such supplementation may be useful during outdoor summer activity, such as football practice. An individual probably should not weight train in a hot, stuffy room. But, if such training is necessary, small doses of Vitamin C may be helpful.

B complex supplementation generally is not necessary. However, individuals on a low calorie diet or an unbalanced diet may require Vitamin B supplementation. In addition, B_{12} supplements may be necessary for vegetarians who avoid animal products.

Mineral supplementation generally is not effective in enhancing exercise performance. However, iron stores in exercising women should be monitored. Iron supplementation may be necessary in some women, but large doses of iron will not enhance performance in the women or men.

SUGGESTED READINGS

1. American College of Sports Medicine. Position stand: the use of anabolic-androgenic steroids in sports. *Medicine and Science in Sports and Exercise* (915): 534-539, 1987.
2. Powers, S.K. and E.T. Howley. *Exercise Physiology: Theory and Application to Fitness and Performance*. Dubuque: Wm. C. Brown, Chapters 18 and 23, 1990.
3. Williams, M.H. *Beyond Training: How Athletes Enhance Performance Legally and Illegally*. Champaign: Leisure Press, 1989.
4. Williams, H.H. *Nutrition and Fitness and Sport*. Dubuque: Wm. C. Brown, 1989.

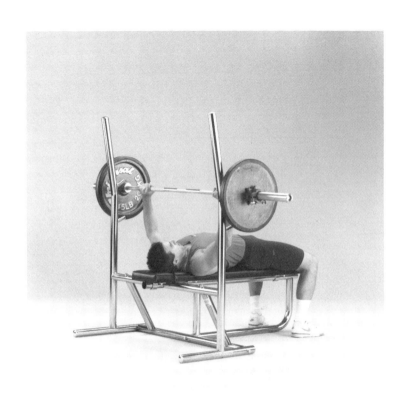

WEIGHT GAIN AND WEIGHT LOSS

Optimal body weight can be a beneficial factor in healthy living as well as in sports performance. Millions of individuals who exercise do so to lose or gain weight. However, gaining or losing weight also can be difficult and dangerous. Generally a conservative, long-term approach is both more effective and safer.

CALORIC BALANCE

For most individuals, weight control depends on the amount of calories (Cal) taken in versus the amount of Cal used.

Caloric Balance =

Caloric Intake - Caloric Output

While this equation is an oversimplification, for the majority of American adults it is a usable estimate of caloric balance. If an individual is in positive caloric balance, he/she eventually will gain weight. If a person is in negative caloric balance, weight eventually will be lost. For example, if a young woman is eating 2600 Cal per day and using 2500 Cal per day, she would have 100 Cal per day positive balance.

2600 Caloric Intake - 2500 Caloric Output

= 100 Caloric Balance

A positive balance of 100 Cal per day (the equivalent of two cookies) would go unnoticed initially even if the individual was weighing frequently. But this positive balance would equal 700 Cal per week and 3500 Cal per five weeks. Since 3500 Cal is equal to about one pound of fat, this individual would gain a pound every five weeks. In one year, about 10 lbs. would be gained. Therefore, even small caloric differences can add up over a long period of time. The term creeping obesity appropriately describes this problem. Of course, caloric balance operates in the opposite direction as well. A consistent negative balance of only 100 Cal per day would equal a weight loss of about 10 lbs. in one year.

Caloric intake relates to nutrients and calories taken into the body. Caloric output refers to expenditure of calories by the body. This expenditure of calories can be divided into three categories (Table 8.1).

A systematic exercise training program will greatly increase weekly caloric expenditure. All types of exercise will burn calories. In general, weight-bearing activities such as jogging and racquetball will burn more calories than nonweight-bearing activities such as cycling and swimming. Resistance training does not use a large amount of calories because much of the time during the session is spent in rest or recovery and often only a small muscle mass is active (e.g., the arms). High intensity lifting does stimulate caloric

Table 8.1. *Caloric Expenditure Per Day in Young Healthy Adults*		
ACTIVITY	CALORIES	
	Male	Female
Basal Metabolic Rate	1500	1200
Routine Daily Activities	2000	1500
Extra Activities-Exercise Training (45 minutes circuit resistance training)	500	400
Total Calories per Day	4000	3100

expenditure for a considerable period of time after the workout. The continuous exercise of circuit resistance training (CRT) enhances energy use, especially fat.

Many nutritionists believe the energy input and output equation is an oversimplification of the complex process of weight control. It is probable that all calories are not alike and that certain kinds of food stimulate the appetite more than others. For example, foods affect appetite depending on how they alter blood insulin levels. Foods which are high in glucose and sucrose (table sugar) cause a surge of insulin secretion which may further stimulate appetite. If this sequence is repeated over months and years, the body will decrease its sensitivity to insulin, the effect of which will stimulate the production of even more insulin and perhaps enhance the appetite. Thus, a "vicious cycle" develops, and overweight individuals find it relatively easy to gain more weight. This insulin theory suggests that restricting the intake of certain kinds of calories may be important to weight control. In addition, other factors can significantly affect the energy balance equation. BMR varies among individuals depending on genetic, lifestyle, and environmental factors. Energy required by the body to process meals, the thermic effect of food (TEF), also is different among individuals. For example, lean individuals have a higher TEF. In addition, some individuals seem to retain more and excrete less calories from the food they eat. This altered "food efficiency" is especially true in individuals on severe diets. The simple caloric balance equation does not account for these energy differences among individuals.

WEIGHT GAIN

Many individuals feel that gaining weight will allow them to perform better in sports. In addition, today's society places a high value on a lean muscular physique; therefore, many individuals want to gain muscular weight for esthetic reasons. With few exceptions, body fat gain is not a goal in an exercise and diet program.

A number of individuals could benefit from weight gain. From the skinny high school freshman to the atrophied elderly adult, increases in muscle mass could improve performance in routine activities as well as in sports. One key to weight gain is <u>adding protein weight without adding fat weight</u>. A second major key is to <u>gain weight without detracting from overall physical fitness</u>.

How Much Gain?

It is difficult to pinpoint exactly how much weight a person can or should gain. Body composition is one criterion which can be used to monitor weight gain. For example, % fat should not exceed the average for your age group (See Appendix D). By monitoring body composition changes, one can ensure that the majority of weight gain is in the form of lean tissue or lean body weight (LBW). A second criterion would be the rate of weight gain. Patience is necessary for any lasting body weight modification. A reasonable goal for weight gain would be to average 0.5 pound per week over a six month period. Gaining 1 pound per week over a three month period is possible but probably not as healthy. Rapid weight gain or weight loss usually can be sustained only for very short periods, and the changes generally are very temporary.

Two tools which will ensure appropriate lean tissue weight gain are: dietary modifications and resistance training. To gain muscle mass, it is imperative that the muscle be provided with amino acids, the protein building blocks. In addition, the muscle must have a stimulus to uptake and incorporate the amino acids. Resistance exercise provides this stimulus. Thus, both dietary and exercise strategies are necessary for increasing lean body weight.

Diet

As discussed in Chapter 7, the RDA for protein (0.8 g/kg/d) can be easily achieved by the sedentary or active man or woman. However, individuals using heavy resistance training, and especially those with weight gain goals, may require as much as 2.5 g/kg/d of "mixed quality" protein intake (Table 8.2). If protein intake is "high quality", i.e., foods containing the essential amino acids, then the requirement may be cut in half. Individuals engaged in heavy exercise should attempt to increase their intake of high quality proteins. Since this strategy means increasing the intake of animal products, excessive fat intake may be a problem. It is important to increase protein intake <u>without</u> substantially increasing fat intake. Table 8.3 indicates foods which are high in protein and low in fat. Notice the grams of protein for each food. Keep in mind that the daily goal for weight gain is around 120 g for normal weight female and 150 g for normal weight male. The need increases as body weight increases. Table 8.4 lists a sample of the foods necessary to meet the targeted protein intake for one day. This list

Table 8.2. *Protein Allowance in Young Adults*

SEDENTARY (RDA)	**Female**	.8 g/kg/day x 55 kg = 44 g/day = 1.5 oz/day
	Male	.8 g/kg/day x 70 kg = 56 g/day = 2.0 oz/day
HEAVY EXERCISE	**Female**	2.2 g/kg/day x 55 kg = 120 g/day = 4.2 oz.day
	Male	2.2 g/kg/day x 70 kg = 150 g/day = 5.4 oz/day

illustrates that the recommended protein dosage would be difficult to obtain each day.

Some problems are associated with high protein intake. Excess protein may be converted to fat which would increase body fat stores (Figure 8.1). This can occur even during moderate protein intake if the muscles are not stimulated to uptake amino acids. Thus individuals on a high protein diet can increase % body fat. Joint inflammation also is a possibility, and the kidneys have an added strain as they excrete by-products of protein metabolism, such as urea. To assist the kidneys, extra quantities of fluid should be consumed during a high protein diet. Because of these potential risks, protein intake should not exceed 2.5 g/kg body weight per day and should approach this quantity only if the individual is engaged in vigorous resistance training at least 4-5 hours per week.

In addition to the 400 Cal of extra protein (+100 g x 4 Cal/g) needed in the diet, the cells also need extra energy to incorporate these amino acids into muscle protein. Extra dietary fat and carbohydrate will provide energy necessary for protein synthesis and fuel for exercise. These foodstuffs can spare protein by reducing the need for protein as an energy source. Thus, less protein will be broken down when fat and CHO intake is adequate.

Increases in dietary fat will naturally accompany the increase in dietary protein. All high quality proteins generally are relatively high in fat. However, dietary CHO requires the special attention of the vigorous exerciser. This foodstuff

Table 8.3. *High Protein-Low Fat Foods*

Food	Amount	Grams Protein	% Protein*	% Fat*
Cheese (lowfat cottage)	1 cup	28	68	11
Milk (1% lowfat)	1 cup	8	32	27
Milk (non-fat, skim)	1 cup	8	32	0
Egg White	1	3	80	0
Clams	3 oz	11	68	14
Oysters	1 cup	20	50	22
Shrimp (boiled)	3 oz	21	84	9
Tuna (canned in water)	3 oz	28	88	7
Beef Roast (lean)	3 oz	25	60	35
Beef Steak (sirloin-lean)	3 oz	27	61	30
Chicken (without skin)	2 pieces	15	80	3
Chicken (fried)	2 pieces	26	58	25
Beans (navy)	1 cup	15	26	4
Beans (lima)	1 cup	13	28	5
Lentils	1 cup	16	30	0
Peas	1 cup	8	20	6

*percentage of total calories

Table 8.4. *Sample Daily Protein Intake of Heavy Exerciser*	

Subject: Male, 20 yrs, 70 kg

Goal: 2.2 g x 70 kg = 154 g/day
616 protein Cal/day

SAMPLE FOODS	GRAMS
skim milk (2 cups)	16
yogurt (2 cups)	16
hamburger (lean 4 oz)	32
chicken (4 oz)	32
eggs (2)	12
macaroni and cheese (1 cup)	18
navy beans (1 cup)	15
peas (1/2 cup)	5
peanut butter (2 tbsp)	8
	154 g

times associated with the exercise. The most critical times are 2-3 days prior to a big event, during the exercise, and 1-2 hours post-exercise. In general, the individual on a daily exercise program needs to eat a substantial amount of carbohydrate with each meal. Although sugars in candy, cake, ice cream, and other sweets provide usable energy, complex CHO found in bread, pasta, potatoes, and beans are more beneficial both in loading the muscle with glycogen and for overall health benefit.

As with protein, one of the problems with "sweets" is that these foods generally have a relatively high fat content. Table 8.5 contains a list of foods with high CHO, low fat composition.

Although the individual needs to concentrate on extra dietary protein and CHO for weight gain, vitamin and mineral supplementation generally is not necessary. The high calorie diet of a weight gain program will provide all necessary vitamins and minerals. Only when the exerciser is following a low calorie diet should such supplementation be considered.

Resistance Training

Like protein intake, heavy resistance training is critical to gaining lean body weight. Once protein is taken into the body, a stimulus must exist to activate amino acid uptake by muscle. Heavy resistance training causes the body to use the amino acids from protein by

is a primary factor in successful exercise performance and, together with fat, will provide the energy necessary for protein rebuilding. It is important for individuals involved in weight gain programs to be sure adequate amounts of CHO exist in the diet. As indicated in Chapter 7, it is especially important that CHO be eaten at certain

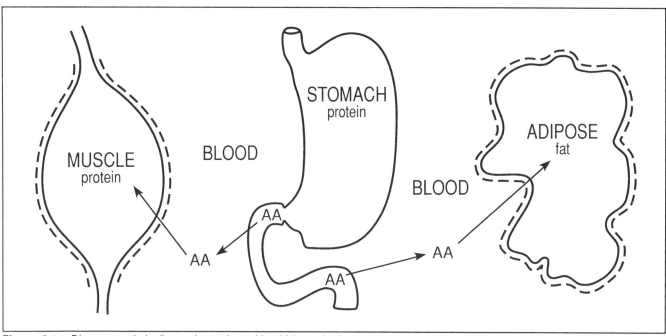

Figure 8.1. *Dietary protein is digested to amino acids which can be incorporated into muscle or fat.*

Table 8.5. *High Carbohydrate - Low Fat Foods*

Food	Amount	Grams CHO	% CHO*	% Fat*
Apple	1 medium	20	99	tr
Applesauce	1 cup	58	100	0
Banana	8 in	26	99	tr
Beans (green)	1 cup	7	80	5
Beans (navy)	1 cup	40	72	5
Biscuits (buttermilk)	2	25	59	37
Blackberries	1 cup	18	94	7
Bread (whole wheat)	1 slice	12	75	16
Cake (angel food)	1 piece	32	95	0
Canteloupe	1	38	96	3
Cereal (bran flakes)	1 oz	28	95	5
Cereal (Golden Grahams)	1 oz	24	87	8
Cereal (Grape Nuts)	1 oz	23	84	0
Cereal (rolled wheat)	1 oz	41	91	5
Cereal (Wheaties)	1 oz	23	92	9
Cereal (oatmeal)	1 oz uncooked	18	72	18
Chili (canned mix)	1/2 cup	18	80	10
Corn (whole kernel)	1/2 cup	18	90	11
Cranberry sauce (canned)	1/4 cup	21	99	tr
Dates	10	58	98	2
Fruit cocktail	1 cup	49	100	0
Fruit punch (Minute Maid)	6 fl oz	23	100	0
Fruitwheats (Nabisco)	1 oz	23	100	0
Gatorade (fruit)	16 fl oz	28	100	0
Gelatin (plain dessert)	1/2 cup	17	97	0
Gingerbread	1 piece	32	74	22
Grapefruit	1	21	98	2
Honey (strained)	1 tbsp	17	100	0
Ice milk	1 cup	29	63	24
Juice (cranberry)	1 cup	41	100	0
Juice (fruit, Welch's)	6 fl oz	22	98	0
Juice, orange	1 cup	26	95	0
Macaroni	1 cup	32	83	3
Mangoes	1 medium	23	10	-
Noodles (egg)	1 cup	37	74	9
Pancakes	2	18	60	30
Pasta	2 oz dry	50	95	4
Peaches (canned, syrup)	1/2 cup	26	96	tr
Pear (raw)	1 medium	5	88	8
Pineapple	1 cup	21	98	2
Pizza (cheese)	1/4 of 12 in	58	68	16
Potato (baked)	1 medium	33	88	tr
Potato (sweet, baked)	1 medium	36	89	6
Pretzels	10	46	78	11
Prunes	2 oz	36	100	0
Pudding (rice with raisins)	1 cup	70	70	18
Pudding (tapioca)	1 cup	28	51	33
Ravioli (beef)	8 oz	36	63	20
Ravioli (mini)	8 oz	31	59	21
Rice (White)	1 cup	0	89	0
Sherbet (orange)	1 cup	60	92	7
Spaghetti	1 cup	39	82	5
Strawberries	1 cup	38	94	6
Watermelon	8 in wedge	27	6	7
Yogurt (fruit)	8 oz	44	73	10

*percentage of total calories

stimulating: 1. the uptake of amino acids by skeletal muscle 2. the manufacture of muscular protein from amino acids 3. net conservation of muscular protein.

The specifics of a resistance training program for strength and bulk are discussed in Chapters 10 and 11. In general, heavy resistances need to be used 4-6 days per week, i.e., 2-3 times per week for each muscle group. The exact number of sets and reps for a weight gain program is debatable, but lifting to failure during each set probably is important. Likewise, each total workout should be fairly exhausting. However, ample time between sessions is critical. The body will require 24-48 hours to rebuild the muscles after a hard workout. Allow plenty of time to let the exercise stimulus perform its function, i.e. build muscle. Two days between sessions using the same muscle may be best; thus, the recommended Monday-Thursday, Tuesday-Friday regimen found in Chapter 11. Do not be afraid to skip a workout due to fatigue or illness.

When All Else Fails

Weight gain (or weight loss) can be a very frustrating exeeperience. Plateaus are common. Athletes especially find they cannot get their weight beyond a certain point. A physical exam may be beneficial to ensure that no disease or disorder is causing weight loss or preventing weight gain. Sometimes an individual feels great, is having great workouts, getting ample dietary protein, and still is gaining little weight. In such cases, one or more of the following recommendations may be attempted:

1. Be patient. Exercise uses calories, so very small positive caloric balances may require several weeks to show up on the scale.
2. Rededicate yourself to the resistance training program. Be especially conscious of program cycling and program pyramiding. Increase the time per session but use each muscle group no more than 3 times per week and on alternate days.
3. Move to a more "body building" program of resistance training. This type of program involves longer sessions using more sets and more repetitions with slightly reduced loads. This is a "high volume" program and may require guidance from an experienced lifter.
4. Concentrate on protein intake. Count the number of grams of protein eaten per day; any bookstore will have a nutrition-calorie

counting booklet. (You might also get one from the state extension office.)
5. Try a protein supplement. Be conservative and follow the guidelines in Table 8.6. Do not substitute a protein supplement for balanced meals. Rather, supplement the balanced meals. As an alternative to a high powered, expensive supplement, a "grocery store" supplement might be equally effective. For example, a well-known instant breakfast (sugar free) when mixed with skim milk provides 15 g of protein per 8 oz drink. Four of these ingested during the day would provide 60g of extra protein in the diet. Research on this topic has been divided on whether protein supplementation enhances strength or lean body weight gains. However, the supplement used in some studies has been of poor quality and low dosage. Amino acids found in supplements are identical to those found in natural foods. However, supplements may not contain the vitamins and minerals which accompany protein in foods. Remember excess protein intake can have side effects; so be cautious.

Any of the five suggestions listed above should produce some gains within one month. Patience is important. Too much too fast will inevitably lead to injury, illness, and very temporary weight gain. A summary of weight gain strategies is found in Table 8.7.

Table 8.6. *Guidelines for a Protein Supplement*

1. All eight essential amino acids (Table 7.1) plus alanine. Scientific research does not support the ingestion of ornithine and arginine to stimulate growth hormone release.

2. No fat content.

3. Moderate carbohydrate content (less than 30% of calories).

4. No vitamin or mineral above the RDA.

5. No fiber.

6. Dose no greater than 1.5 g/kg/day (if 100% protein, 1.5 g x body weight = g of supplement maximum).

7. Taken with extra fluids.

Table 8.7.	Summary: Lean Body Weight Gain Programs

1. Heavy resistance training is a key to muscular weight gain.

2. When involved in heavy resistance training, protein intake should approach 2g/kg/day but no more than 2.5 g/kg/day.

3. Intake of foods with complete or high quality proteins is preferred.

4. Resistance training can be intensified using strategies with cycles and pyramids.

5. A protein supplement containing essential amino acids and alanine may be beneficial if the diet contains insufficient high quality protein.

6. Protein intake in excess of the body's needs can lead to health problems including overfatness.

7. Routine aerobic exercise will help decrease or maintain body fat and improve overall conditioning.

performed for one or two weeks can help an individual identify where dietary or activity lifestyle practices need to be altered. Most comprehensive nutrition books provide a list of foods and calories and most exercise physiology texts provide a table of the caloric cost of common daily activities and exercises. (See Suggested Readings at the end of Chapters 7 and 8.)

A reasonable weight loss goal would be an average of 1 lb per week over a three month period. Losing 3% of body weight in less than one week has been shown to be detrimental to the CV system and to exercise performance. Body composition can be a criterion for the limit of weight loss. Percent body fat should always exceed 5% in men and 10% in women. Since the accuracy of body composition analysis is usually questionable, a safety margin of +2% is advisable (7% men, 12% women).

Reducing Caloric Intake

For muscular tone, some weight loss may be necessary. Crash dieting is one way of obtaining negative caloric balance. However, weight reduction by this method is very transient. If an extreme diet is attempted for more than a few days, serious health problems can result. Food restriction diets do not provide the essential amino acids or vitamins and minerals necessary for

WEIGHT LOSS

The majority of American adults can be considered overweight to some degree. Weight loss or weight maintenance is one of the most cited motivational factors by individuals initiating an exercise program. Recently the definition of overweight and optimal weight have been examined by various researchers and professional groups. Many fitness experts support the concept that the amount of body fat rather than total body weight is the key indicator of an individual's fitness status. Thus the term "overfat" has evolved, and a plethora of techniques have been developed to lose body fat. Some evidence does point to potential health problems associated with "hypermuscularity" and excess body weight of any composition (Figure 8.2)

The process of determining the amount of caloric intake or output each day, calorie counting, is a very tedious and time consuming undertaking. Yet, such an activity carefully

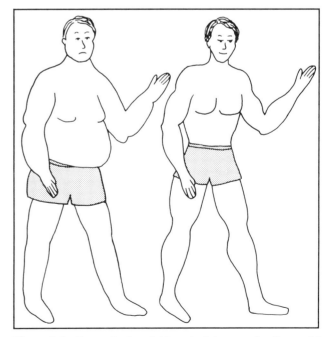

Figure 8.2. *Excess body weight can be fat or muscle. Excess fat weight is more unhealthy. Large amounts of abdominal fat can be expecially dangerous.*

67

proper body function. In addition to health hazards, food restriction causes the loss of body water. In fact, most of the weight lost during a rapid (less than one week) diet regimen is water, which can account for as much as 70% of the weight loss during the initial few days. As the negative caloric balance continues over three to four weeks, water loss contributes progressively less while fat becomes the major constituent of the lost weight. Therefore, weight reduction by negative caloric balance is physiologically more beneficial if done slowly. Even when weight is lost slowly by caloric restriction, some body protein is part of the lost weight.

Rather than crash dieting, more permanent eating habit changes are necessary in order to ensure safe, permanent weight control. Reducing total caloric intake to a reasonable level, an amount that can be maintained indefinitely, is probably the best strategy in planning a dietary program. Foods which are high in carbohydrate, especially simple sugars, and fats should be reduced. The substitution of foods high in protein is not always beneficial, because many protein sources, such as meat and eggs, also can have a high fat content. Thus, the reduction of calories should be from carbohydrate, fat, and protein. Increasing foods high in fiber, such as vegetables, grains, and fruits, can increase the bulk in the diet and help reduce the total caloric intake while still producing the feeling of fullness or satiety. Other possible dietary changes include eating more fish and lean meats, such as grass fattened cattle, poultry, and wild game, and reducing the intake of eggs and whole milk products. Use of skim or half percent milk by adults will reduce fat intake and still provide substantial EAA, vitamins, and minerals. Substituting desserts which are higher in complex carbohdyrate and other nutrients and reducing desserts high in simple carbohdyrate is another beneficial strategy. Pies, cookies, and cakes are composed almost solely of simple sugars. Substitutions of fresh fruit or whole grain desserts generally will provide fewer calories, more nutrients, and an adequate feeling of satiety.

Calories from beverages also need to be considered. Soft drink consumption has risen dramatically over the past several years, especially in children. All sweetened soft drinks are high in calories because of their high sugar content (Table 8.8). Furthermore, such drinks are usually void of any nutrients. Low calorie drinks or water can be substituted for sugar sweetened soft drinks. The long-term risks of the sweetener aspartame have not been fully evaluated. Alcoholic beverages can be surprisingly high in calories (Table 8.8). Not only is alcohol itself

Table 8.8. *High Calorie Beverages*	
BEVERAGE	**CALORIES**
Soft Drinks	
Colas (12 oz)	150
Root Beer (12 oz)	150
Fruit Flavored Sodas (12 oz)	170
Ginger Ale (12 oz)	115
Alcoholic Beverages and Mixes	
Whiskey, Gin, Rum, Vodka, Scotch (1.5 oz.)	
100 proof	125
80 proof	100
Tom Collins Mix (8 oz.)	300
Daiquiri Mix (8 oz.)	175
Whiskey Sour Mix (8 oz.)	175
Tomato Juice (8 oz.)	50
Beer (12 oz.)	150
Light Beer (12 oz.)	75-125
Wines	
Table (3.5 oz.)	85
Dessert (3.5 oz.)	140
Cooler (3.5 oz.)	100

calorific but the mixes used in liquor consumption also are high in calories and sugar content. Low calorie beverages include water, diet soft drinks, unsweetened tea and coffee, lightly sweetened lemonade, and skim milk.

Some research evidence suggests that the daily caloric consumption should be spread out in evenly spaced small meals. For a given caloric intake, 3-5 smaller daily meals are more beneficial than 1-2 large meals. "High meal frequency" is associated with lower body weight, smaller skinfold thickness, and lower blood cholesterol. When only one large meal per day is consumed, an evening meal tends to produce weight gain while eating the majority of calories at breakfast induces a weight loss. These findings would suggest that the common practice of obtaining the majority of the daily calories in a large evening meal makes weight loss more difficult.

Individuals involved in resistance training require additional vitamins, minerals, and calories to support their extra activity. Therefore, caloric restriction can cause reduction in exercise performance and even nutritional deficiencies. The exerciser must use caution in restricting calories over a prolonged period of time. A multivitamin and mineral supplement may be advantageous but should contain no more than 100% of the RDA for each nutrient. For example, the RDA for iron in a young adult female is 15 mg; therefore, a supplement should contain a maximum of 15 mg (Table 8.9).

Likewise, protein requirements are increased during resistance training. Intake of high quality protein should include foods low in fat (Table 8.3). In addition, non-animal products can be eaten to ensure a lower caloric intake. Since vegetables are not complete proteins, it is necessary to use combinations of vegetable products so that all EAA are eaten together (Table 8.10).

Since exercise performance is dependent on muscle stores of glycogen, CHO intake must be maintained even on a low calorie diet. If CHO intake is inadequate, fuel sources for resistance exercise will be more rapidly depleted, leading to early discomfort and fatigue. Glycogen stores can be maintained by eating foods high in CHO and low in fat (Table 8.5) at most if not all regular meals. In addition, ingesting dilute CHO fluids during exercise and CHO snacks immediately following exercise is beneficial.

Table 8.10. *Examples of Food Combinaions for Essential Amino Acids**
baked beans and whole wheat bread rice and bean casserole corn tortillas and refried beans pea soup and whole grain bread peanut butter sandwich pinto beans and corn bread kidney beans and corn bread
*in general a grain is combined with a legume

The use of laxatives and diuretics for weight loss is dangerous for anyone but especially for the individual involved in physical training. These practices deplete stores of body fluids and a number of minerals. Weight loss from such methods is very temporary, and exercise performance almost always is reduced. Such extreme measures as these generally are counterproductive to the long-term weight loss goals of the program and to the health of the individual.

Resistance Training

Resistance training is generally not the most effective type of exercise to promote weight loss. Heavy lifting certainly burns calories but actually not as many as prolonged, vigorous aerobic exercise. This difference probably is due to the frequent rest periods associated with resistance exercise. Therefore, one strategy for losing weight is to shorten or eliminate the rest periods. For example, in circuit resistance training, the rest periods between stations are abbreviated to 15 seconds. The rest period can be completely eliminated by incorporating one or more aerobic modes into the circuit. (See Chapter 11 for specific examples.) By performing an aerobic exercise in place of the rest period, the caloric expenditure during each resistance training session can be greatly increased. A vigorous CRT program of 30 min each session, performed three times per week can contribute an additional 1200-1500 Cal to the weekly energy expenditure. Athletes training for sports competition can use as much as 5000-7500 Cal per week due to the exercise. It is obvious that an individual is much more likely to be in negative or equal caloric balance if an exercise training program is part of the regular lifestyle.

Table 8.9. *RDA for Young Adults**

	Men	Women
Vitamin		
A	1000 mg	800 mg
D	10 mg	10 mg
E	10 mg	8 mg
K	80 mg	60 mg
C	60 mg	60 mg
thiamin	1.5 mg	1.1 mg
riboflavin	1.7 mg	1.3 mg
niacin	19 mg	15 mg
B6	2 mg	1.6 mg
folate	200 mg	180 mg
B12	2 mg	2 mg
Mineral		
calcium	800 mg	1200 mg
phosphorus	800 mg	1200 mg
magnesium	350 mg	280 mg
iron	10 mg	15 mg
zinc	15 mg	12 mg
iodine	150 mg	150 mg
selenium	70 mg	55 mg

*Ages 19-24 years

As discussed earlier, resistance training stimulates protein build-up in muscle. This "supercompensation" has the tendency to promote weight gain. Such effect would favorably alter body composition, but not promote weight loss. To reduce this stimulus, lighter loads should be used during the workout. Lifting to failure also should be avoided because such efforts probably lead to enhanced protein breakdown and then rebuilding. A circuit resistance training program with its lighter loads (40-60% RM) offers the type of resistance exercise which might best reduce body weight.

In addition to traditional CRT workouts, more prolonged exercise sessions may stimulate greater use of fat as an energy source. Thus, multiple sets and a more prolonged aerobic component may assist in beneficially altering body composition through fat weight loss. Exercise sessions of 60-90 min in duration also may promote greater energy expenditure in recovery. Some research studies have demonstrated that additional energy is used for as much as 24 hours after prolonged vigorous exercise (Figure 1.4). Such a residual effect could have significant impact on weight loss over a period of time. Vigorous game-type activities, such as racketball and basketball also can be high calorie burners and can stimulate extra calorie burning in recovery. A key to using such activities in the weight loss program is to reduce the rest periods, i.e., stand-around time: jog after errant balls, start play quickly following breaks in the action, etc. Table 8.11 summarizes the general recommendations for weight loss programs.

Spot Reduction

Often an individual desires to lose fat from a specific area of the body. Continuous aerobic exercise is the best technique to stimulate fat burning. Heavy resistance weight training does not use fat as a primary energy source although fat is used during the recovery period following a resistance exercise session. Circuit resistance training, which is more continuous exercise, has been shown to reduce body fat stores and decrease percent body fat.

Abdominal fat is especially important to lose because individuals with large fat deposits in the stomach are more susceptible to cardiovascular disease. Fortunately, abdominal fat is one of the preferred sites for fat mobilization during exercise. That is, fat stored around the stomach is transferred to the blood and used by working muscles during prolonged exercise. On

Table 8.11. *Summary: Weight Loss Programs*
1. Avoid rapid weight loss.
2. Lose weight over an extended period with a goal of 2 lbs/week maximum.
3. Avoid weight cycling (continual loss and gain of weight). Stay within 5 lbs of desired weight.
4. Rely on exercise rather than food restriction as much as possible.
5. Use CRT and prolonged exercise to increase caloric expenditure.
6. Avoid the use of vomiting, laxatives, diuretics which complicate dehydration and dramatically affect health and performance.
7. Rehydrate whenever possible with low calorie drinks.
8. Vitamin and mineral supplementation may be necessary but should not exceed the RDA.
9. Determine minimal weight using established equations, with body fat minimum at 7% for men and 12% for women.
10. Maintain carbohydrate intake, especially immediately following exercise and between events.

the other hand, the fat in the thigh region is more resistant to mobilization and thus harder to lose.

If one area of the body is especially fat, it is tempting to exercise that region hard in an effort to lose the fat. Some scientific research supports the idea of "spot reduction" but other research does not. Certainly by exercising the muscle of the target area, the region will look and feel firmer. Some loss of fat may occur by exercising a specific area, e.g., numerous sit-ups to affect abdominal fat. However, a more effective method of "toning" an area is to combine prolonged aerobic exercise with moderate dietary restriction and specific resistance exercises. Using this combination of exercise and diet, both local muscle tone and regional fat stores will be affected beneficially.

SUGGESTED READINGS

1. Katch, F.L. and W.D. McArdle. *Nutrition, Weight, and Exercise*. Philadelphia: Lea & Febiger, Chapters 5, 6, 7, and 8, 1988.

2. Williams, M.H. *Nutrition for Fitness and Sport*. Dubuque: W.C. Brown, Chapters 5, 6, 7, 9, 10, and 11, 1988.

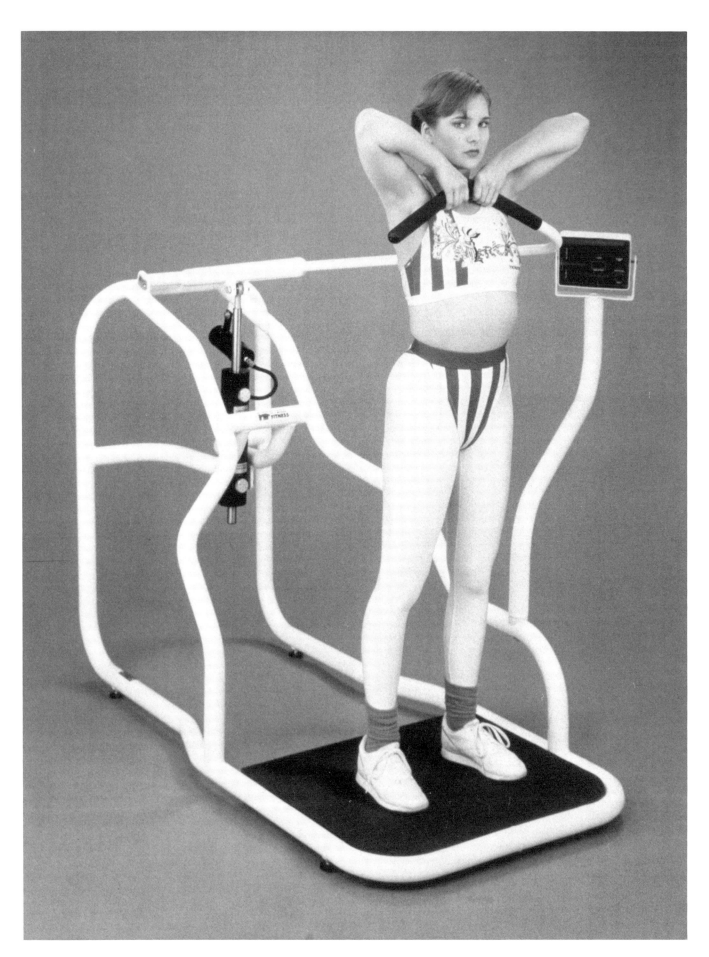

RESISTANCE TRAINING FOR WOMEN

Perhaps no other aspect of the fitness boom has had a greater effect on the exercise habits of women than the increased use of weight equipment by this sex. Even gyms previously reserved for men who were involved in very heavy resistance training now find women among their clientele. Women have found that their muscles, like those of men, adapt well to the stimulus of resistance training. In fact, the muscle fibers of men and women are very similar in basic structure and function. However, the male muscle is often larger, and the differences between the sexes in "lean body weight" (bone and muscle) affects performance in many activities including resistance training. In addition, the reproductive cycle and pregnancy cause a need for special considerations in planning the resistance programs for women.

STRENGTH AND HYPERTROPHY

After puberty, males exhibit greater strength than females in virtually all muscles. Much of this difference is simply due to the larger muscle of the man rather than any innate strength characteristic of the male muscle fiber. However, some of the strength difference has been attributed to a lack of exercise and sports' participation by females in the teen years. With female sports participation now increasing, the magnitude of strength differences is declining. The absolute strength gains for muscle groups trained with resistance exercises is lower in females. Males will gain extra strength because of their greater capacity to add muscular bulk.

The capacity for muscular enlargement or hypertrophy is less in females because of lower production of the hormone testosterone. Some women with naturally higher testosterone levels have a greater ability to stimulate muscular hypertrophy. Anabolic steroids potentially are more effective in women. (See Chapter 7.) However, the risks also are greater in women including the alteration of sexual characteristics.

Females can gain some muscular size increases with resistance training. A larger and firmer muscle produces the muscular tone which is a goal of many exercise programs. Exercises, such as aerobics and circuit resistance training, decrease subcutaneous fat and enhance muscular tone.

Perhaps the largest difference between untrained male and female performance is in the area of upper body strength. In some cases, females exhibit only 45% of the absolute strength of males for muscle groups in the arms, shoulders, and chest (Figure 9.1). Even when expressed relative to body weight, the upper body strength of females is about 55% of the males. This is an area in which women can show marked improvement with strength training. In contrast, females compare more favorably to males in lower body strength. In fact, the difference in strength disappears when expressed per kg of body weight (Figure 9.1). The discrepancy between upper and lower body strength in the female suggests that she utilizes the lower body musculature, e.g., in walking, running, etc., more than the upper body musculature.

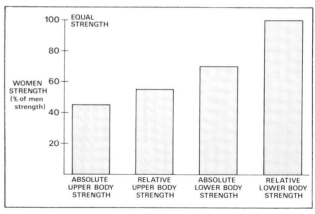

Figure 9.1. *Absolute and relative muscular strength of women compared to men. Absolute strength is the total amount of weight which can be lifted. Relative strength is the amount of weight lifted in relation to body weight.*

Females are able to enhance muscular strength with resistance training. Because the female often begins the training program at a lower level than the male, the "percent improvement" due to the strength training is sometimes greater (Figure 9.2).

When corrected for body weight, isokinetic strength and power are similar in men and women. Some scientific research suggests

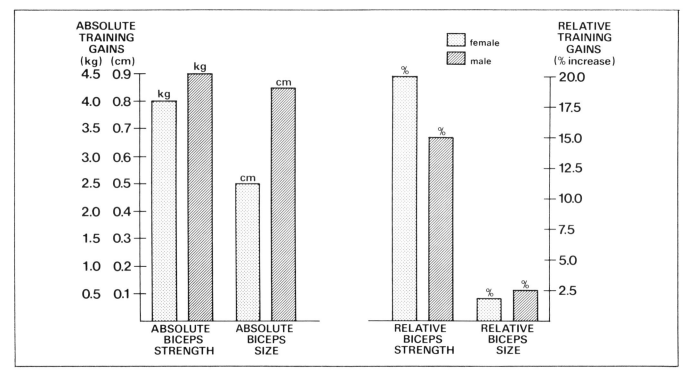

Figure 9.2. *Absolute and relative muscular strength and size gains of women and men caused by a resistance training program. Absolute gains are the amount of increase in strength or girth, and relative gains are the amount of increase in relation to the starting values.*

that men can generate more work at fast speeds of movement. Muscular balance is similar in men and women. That is, in both sexes the hamstrings should equal 60-70% of the strength of the quadriceps at slow contracting speeds. (See Chapter 3.) Likewise, quadriceps and hamstrings muscle groups on each side should be nearly equal in strength.

Metabolism during resistance exercise is similar in men and women. The capabilities of the muscle to use ATP and CP is not related to sex. However, in trained individuals, male muscle appears to be capable of storing larger amounts of glycogen and utilizing fat slightly better than female muscle. This may be a beneficial factor in prolonged training bouts or competitive performance.

Body composition values are presented in Table D.3, Appendix D. The female hormones progesterone and estrogen cause more fat to be deposited in female adipose tissue. This amounts to about 6% additional body fat in the female than in the male. The average values for young adult females and males is 22% and 12% fat, respectively. During aging, women and men add approximately similar amounts of fat, about 1% for every three years. Part of this decline is due to the decrease in bone and muscle density which occurs at about the same rate with age in both sexes. Additional adipose tissue is beneficial in some swimming activities

since fat would assist to buoy-up the body. However, the added weight is probably detrimental to performance in weight-bearing activities such as running and jumping.

EXERCISE AND REPRODUCTIVE FUNCTION

In addition to the physiological differences between women and men, other factors may be important to consider when establishing exercise training programs for females. Most of these factors relate to the physiological and hormonal changes which occur monthly in women.

Reproductive Cycle

The onset of the female reproductive cycle called menarche is often later in the young athlete than the non-athlete. This average age difference has been reported to be as much as two years. The cause or the ramifications of this delay is unknown, but it may be caused by the physical and emotional stress of exercise training and/or by the lower amounts of body fat found in these active girls.

Painful menstruation called "dysmenorrhea" is a frequently reported problem of female athletes. The physiological response to exercise generally is not affected during menstruation, and exercise probably neither causes or cures dysmenorrhea. It is doubtful that physical activity during menstruation results in any physiological damage or danger. Some reports do suggest that active women have less painful menstrual phases and that abdominal strength may be a beneficial factor. Individual variation among women is great, but usually resistance exercises should be avoided or the intensity reduced if dysmenorrhea occurs.

A reduction in the frequency of menstruation is termed "oligomenorrhea," while the complete cessation of menstruation is called "amenorrhea." Such cycle irregularities may relate to body weight and body fat stores. The additional adipose tissue in the female apparently is necessary for normal reproductive capabilities. If body weight becomes too low or training intensity too great, the reproductive cycle may cease. Female gymnasts, dancers, runners, and joggers have greater incidence of amenorrhea than sedentary women. The incidence of amenorrhea is directly related to the amount of training. For example, the cessation of the menstrual cycle is more common in women running 60 miles per week than in those running 20 miles per week. A higher than normal occurrence of amenorrhea also has been reported in female gymnasts, dancers, and swimmers, athletes who train very intensely and often have low body fat values. Little research has been performed using elite female body builders. Because of the training intensity and low body fat, these individuals may be susceptible to interruptions in the menstrual cycle. Greatly diminished levels of sex hormone output are associated with amenorrhea. This disorder appears to be somewhat transient and when training is reduced or eliminated, normal cycling usually returns. The long-term consequences of exercise-induced amenorrhea are unknown.

Because of menstruation, females are more susceptible to iron deficiency than are males. Although many foods contain iron (liver, oysters, apricots, and peaches), it is difficult for most women to obtain the required 15 mg of iron every day. Phytins and other chelating compounds found in vegetables bind the iron and thus reduce its absorption. Hence heme iron from meats is more readily absorbed than non-heme iron found in vegetables. In addition, numerous other dietary components affect iron absorption. For example, vitamin C and calcium increase iron absorption. Exercising may increase the iron requirement. For these reasons, many active women take iron supplementation. If iron is taken in excess over prolonged periods, the stores can build up and become toxic. While this problem is rare in women, it does suggest that hematocrit, hemoglobin, and iron stores' analysis should be performed before prolonged iron supplementation is utilized.

Little is known about the effects of birth control pills on exercise performance. Exogenous estrogens and progesterones are constituents of the pill, and these hormones have effects on energy metabolism, water retention, and dysmenorrhea, all of which might alter the female's response to exercise. Some scientific evidence suggests that use of the pill is associated with decreased muscular strength and endurance.

Pregnancy

Worldwide statistics support the concept that physical activity is excellent preparation for the rigors of childbirth. Active women generally have shorter and less complicated deliveries than sedentary women. Physical conditioning prior to pregnancy may be especially helpful for the mother-to-be. Mild exercise training during pregnancy also is condoned by most scientists and physicians. Activity during pregnancy maintains the physical conditioning of the female and assists in preventing large gains in body weight. After pregnancy, the active woman generally is able to lose the extra weight and regain the pre-pregnancy figure more rapidly.

The fetus is well protected by the uterus and amniotic fluid which can absorb the shocks that occur during exercise. However, vigorous exercise during pregnancy can reduce blood flow to the fetus. In animals, exercise for more than 30 minutes per day by a mother, reduced the birth weight of the offspring.

High intensity exercise during the third trimester (last three months) of pregnancy also can be disadvantageous to the mother. Bouncing movements associated with jogging and lifting can stretch the enlarged breasts and abdominal regions and could cause tissue damage. In addition, intense activity in late pregnancy can compromise the mother's cardiovascular system. The fetal circulation increases the demands on the mother's heart, and during exercise these demands are further enhanced. The mother's heart generally is capable of meeting the extra requirements, but in vigorous, upright exercise, the fetus itself may obstruct venous return coming from the lower extremities of the mother. Thus, the blood arriving at the heart would decrease and subsequently the heart's output would be reduced. This effect is greater as the fetus grows.

Resistance training can affect dramatically the cardiovascular function of the pregnant woman. Elevations in blood pressure caused by resistance exercise can be especially dangerous during pregnancy. For this reason heavy resistance training is not recommended during the last six months of pregnancy. Excessive exercise of any kind should be curtailed by the pregnant woman. However, light exercise may be very beneficial. Low intensity walking, cycling, rowing, swimming, and circuit resistance training with light loads would be acceptable forms of exercise, especially during the later stages of pregnancy.

RESISTANCE EXERCISES

The principles of training muscles are similar for women and men. Specific resistance training programs are presented in Chapter 11. Many women may want to modify these programs for their specific goals.

General Fitness

A circuit resistance program would be very satisfactory for women seeking general fitness and muscular tone. Some women may simply want to add an additional abdominal or thigh exercise to the CRT routine. In addition the incline sit-ups, knee raises, and knee lift exercises can be performed every day for those seeking additional trunk toning and fitness. A good general fitness program for women would be:

Monday — Rhythmic aerobics or other continuous aerobic activity — 40 minutes (not including stretching, warm-up, and cool-down).

Tuesday — Circuit resistance training — 45 minutes.

Wednesday — Rhythmic aerobics or other continuous aerobic activity — 30 minutes.

Thursday — Circuit resistance training — 40 minutes.

Friday — Rhythmic aerobics or other continuous aerobic activity — 40 minutes.

Saturday — (Optional) Circuit resistance training — 30 minutes.

Monday through Saturday — Incline sit-ups (or abdominal curl), knee raises, knee lifts.

Strength and Hypertrophy

The heavy resistance program described in Chapter 11 is designed to maximize strength and enlargement gains. This program may be unnecessarily intense for women and men in certain sports. Some type of "cycling" or varying the intensity is recommended for all heavy resistance programs. For sports such as volleyball, tennis, and basketball, the loads of the program described in Chapter 11 can be reduced by 5% on each set in each phase. Such a reduction will assist in preventing injury and avoiding fatigue. The resulting loads still will provide the muscle with a substantial strength and hypertrophy stimulus.

Heavy resistance exercise in which loads of 75 to 90% of 1RM are used should be reserved for young women who need maximal strength for athletic competition. The circuit resistance training regimen is recommended for women interested in general fitness, muscular tone, and moderate strength gains.

SUGGESTED READINGS

1. Fox, E.L., and D.K. Mathews. *The Physiological Basis of Physical Education and Athletics.* Philadelphia: Saunders, Chapter 14, 1988.
2. Gauthier, M.M. Guidelines for exercise during pregnancy: too little or too much? *Physician and Sportsmedicine.* 14:162-169, April, 1986.
3. Riley, D.P. and J.A. Peterson. *Strength Training for Women.* West Point: Leisure Press, 1981.

RESISTANCE TRAINING FOR SPECIFIC MUSCLE GROUPS

CHAPTER 10

GENERAL GUIDELINES

The principles related to muscular development are presented in Chapters 1, 2, and 3. Resistance training programs for specific activities are described in Chapter 11. Basically resistance training can be used for five purposes: 1. maximal strength and bulk, 2. power training, 3. body building, 4. adequate strength and tone, 5. cardiovascular fitness. Maximal strength and power exercises relate to training for competitive athletics and competitive weight lifting. Resistance training for competitive athletics is described in the next chapter. Body building requires very high volume resistance training with numerous repetitions and sets for each exercise. Adequate strength and tone exercises as well as cardiovascular exercises are for general fitness seekers who are training for lifetime fitness. This type of resistance training is discussed in the next chapter. Regardless of the goal of the exercise, some general guidelines can be used. These are listed in Table 10.1.

MAJOR MUSCLES

One of the most important principles governing resistance training is using the right exercise for the right muscle. A guide to the major muscles is given in Figure 10.1. Many other muscles exist in the body, and for a more detailed picture see an anatomy text. First the muscles used in a given activity must be identified. After proper identification, specific exercises must be chosen which will affect the desired muscles. Exercises which use opposite or antagonistic muscle groups also must be selected. In the general fitness program, a variety of resistance exercises should be selected with emphasis on those muscles which are less active in the aerobic exercises used in the fitness program.

Table 10.1. *General Principles for Effective Resistance Training*

1. Move the resistance through the *full range of motion.*

2. Breathe during each phase of the lift to prevent large increases of intrathoracic pressure.

3. Know the muscle(s) affected by the exercise.

4. Exercise antagonistic muscles to avoid imbalance. For example, quadriceps exercises should be accompanied by hamstrings exercises and pectoralis exercises accompanied by exercises using the upper back muscles such as the infraspinatus, posterior deltoid, and teres minor.

5. Stretch the active muscle and joints *before and after* exercise to prevent loss of flexibility.

6. Warm-up with calisthenics and light lifting before the workout. Cool-down with similar light exercises after the workout.

7. Do not exercise just after eating.

8. Do not use the same muscle in sequential exercises. For example, do not perform the shoulder press and bench press in sequence because both use the triceps extensively.

9. Heavy lifting (75-100% of maximum) is reserved for competitive athletes and weight lifters.

10. After their competitive careers, athletes need to reduce resistance training loads and intensity.

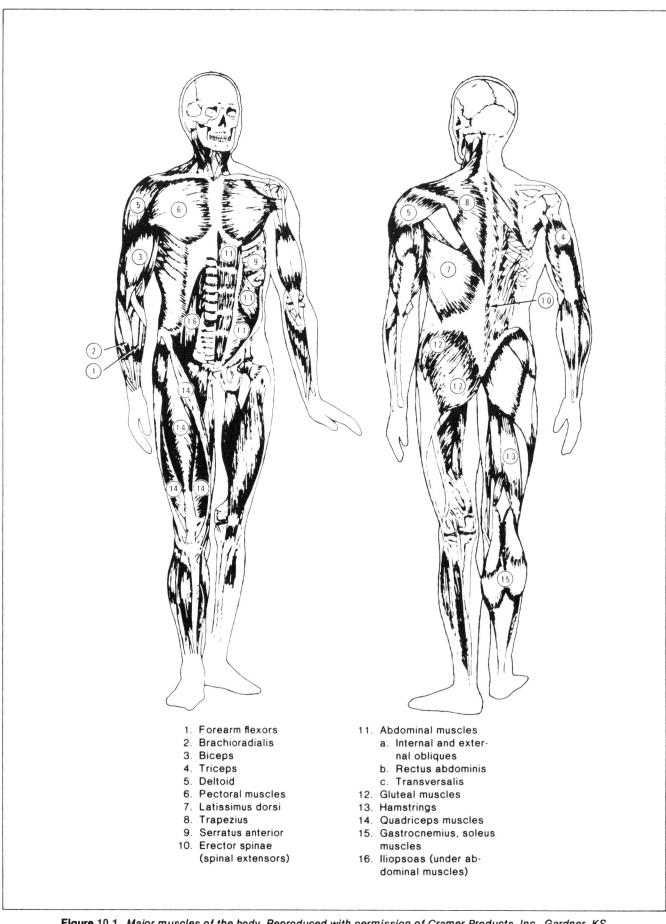

1. Forearm flexors
2. Brachioradialis
3. Biceps
4. Triceps
5. Deltoid
6. Pectoral muscles
7. Latissimus dorsi
8. Trapezius
9. Serratus anterior
10. Erector spinae (spinal extensors)
11. Abdominal muscles
  a. Internal and external obliques
  b. Rectus abdominis
  c. Transversalis
12. Gluteal muscles
13. Hamstrings
14. Quadriceps muscles
15. Gastrocnemius, soleus muscles
16. Iliopsoas (under abdominal muscles)

Figure 10.1. *Major muscles of the body. Reproduced with permission of Cramer Products, Inc., Gardner, KS.*

EXERCISING USING DIFFERENT RESISTANCE MECHANISMS

Virtually any method of providing overload resistance for contraction will produce muscular development and improve muscular function. Presented in the following illustrations are resistance devices using different mechanisms to provide resistance for muscular contraction. The muscles used with the exercise are listed below each illustration. Additional instructions and information on other resistance machines can be obtained from each company.

Free-Weight Resistance

Barbells and dumbells provide a near constant resistance. These weights or loads do not change during the lift. The resistance "felt" by the muscle does change depending on the momentum of the free-weight and the leverage system within the muscle. For example, a 100 lb barbell does not feel like 100 lb to the muscle at all points in the range of motion. It "feels" heavier at the weakest points in the range of motion. In addition, because the muscle must overcome "inertia" at the start of the exercise when the weight is motionless, it requires more force to move the weight than at the end of the lift when the weight is moving and providing "momentum." So the "effective resistance" does vary somewhat in free-weight exercise. However, the variation is not consistent and does not correspond to the muscular strength curves. Still, free-weights are proven means of overloading muscle and producing strength and hypertrophy gains. Free weights offer the advantages of portability and space savings. In addition, they provide good contralateral (opposite limb) resistance. That is, both sides must work equally. Greater skill is required for using free-weights than machines. In addition, the risk of injury is greater because of the potential for dropping the bar or weight. Therefore, the use of free-weights is recommended only for experienced lifters and when assistance (partner) is available.

Photos used in Figures 10.2 to 10.7 and 10.9 were provided by Universal, P.O. Box 1270, Cedar Rapids, IA 52406.

Figure 10.2. *Dumbell arm curl on incline bench. [biceps, brachialis, forearm muscles]*

Figure 10.3. *Arm curl on preacher's curl bench. [biceps, brachialis, forearm muscles] Reverse grip (overhand). [brachioradialis, biceps]*

79

Figure 10.4. *Chest press on supine bench. [pectoralis, deltoids, triceps]*

Figure 10.6. *Shoulder press using behind the neck bench. [deltoids (especially posterior), triceps, trapezius]*

Figure 10.5. *Shoulder press on incline bench. [deltoids (especially anterior), triceps, trapezius]*

Figure 10.7. *Bent-over row using olympic level bar. [trapezius, latissimus dorsi, posterior deltoids, rhomboids, biceps, brachioradialis]*

Figure 10.8. *Upright row. [deltoids, trapezius, biceps, brachioradialis]*

Figure 10.10. *Heel raise. [gastrocnemius, soleus]*

Figure 10.9. *Leg squat using Smith rack. [quadriceps, gluteal muscles, upper hamstrings] Note: For muscular balance, leg curls need to be performed on a machine to train the hamstrings.*

Universal Variable Resistance

The Universal Centurion Dynamic Variable Resistance (DVR) machines provide changes in the load through the range of motion by two mechanisms. In some instruments, the resistance is gradually increased from the start of the movement to the end of the range of motion by altering the resistance arm of the machine lever (Figure 2.3, e.g., Figure 10.12 and 10.14). The change in resistance is reversed during the eccentric phase or return movement. In addition, certain Centurion DVR machines use a multiple cam system so that the resistance is varied depending on the part of the cam that the pully rides. The larger parts of the cam provide greater resistance than the smaller parts (See Figure 10.11 and 10.22). These instruments provide resistance for both concentric and eccentric contractions in each exercise.

Photos used in Figures 10.11 to 10.25 were provided by Universal, P.O. Box 1270, Cedar Rapids, IA 52406. The photos illustrate variable resistance exercise unless otherwise noted.

Figure 10.11. *Arm curl (Centurion). [biceps, brachialis, forearm muscles]*

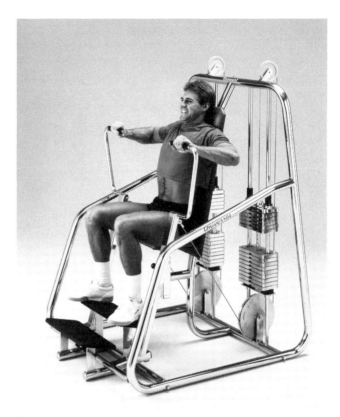

Figure 10.13. *Seated chest press (Centurion). (Seat adjustable to emphasize upper, middle, or lower pectorals.) [pectorals, deltoids, triceps]*

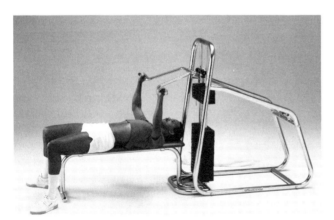

Figure 10.12. *Chest press (Centurion). [pectorals, deltoids, triceps]*

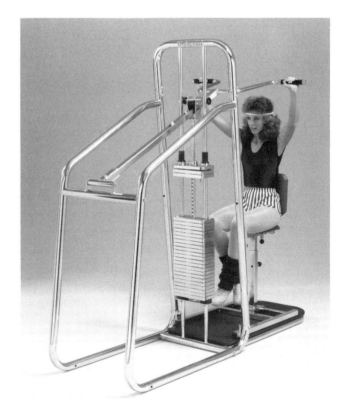

Figure 10.14. *Shoulder press (Centurion). [deltoids, triceps, trapezius]*

Figure 10.15. *Vertical chest butterfly (Centurion). [pectorals, anterior deltoid]*

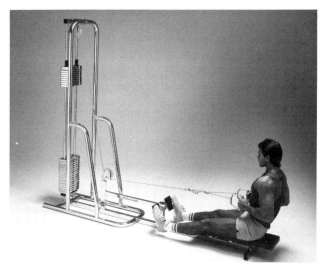

Figure 10.17. *Seated rowing with constant resistance. (trapezius, posterior deltoid, rhomboids, biceps, brachioradialis]*

Figure 10.17A. *Arm curl (left) [biceps, brachialis, forearm muscles] Arm extension (right) [triceps] constant resistance*

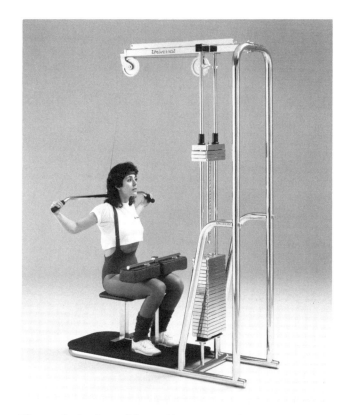

Figure 10.16. *Lat pulldown with constant resistance. [latissimus dorsi, biceps, brachioradialis]*

Figure 10.18. *Abdominal curl using Abdominal Crunch machine with constant resistance. [rectus abdominus, obliques]*

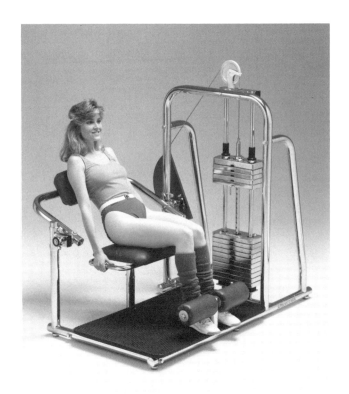

Figure 10.19. *Seated back extension. [erector spinae, gluteals]*

Figure 10.21. *Leg squat (Centurion). [quadriceps, gluteals, upper hamstrings] Calf raises can be performed by extending up onto toes. [gastrocnemius, soleus, pereneals]*

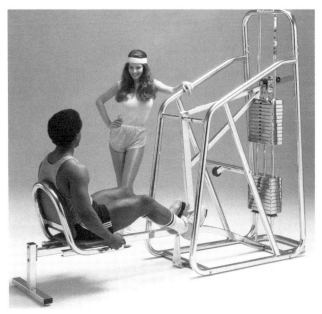

Figure 10.20. *Leg press (Centurion). [quadriceps, gluteals]*

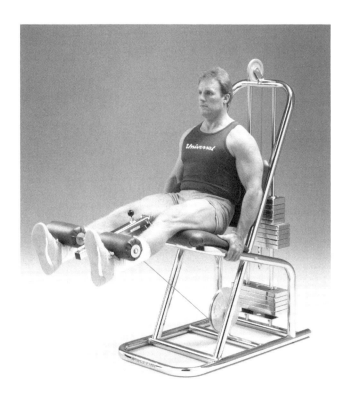

Figure 10.22. *Leg extension (Centurion). [quadriceps]*

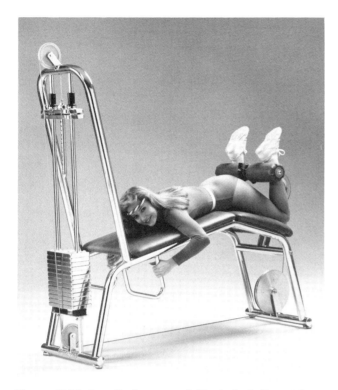

Figure 10.23. *Leg flexion or curl (Centurion). [hamstrings, upper gastrocnemius]*

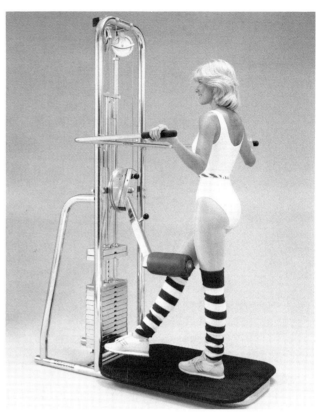

Figure 10.25. *Hip adduction on Total Hip machine. [inner thigh muscles] Hip abduction also can be performed on this machine. [outer thigh muscles, gluteus maximus]*

Figure 10.24. *Hip extension on Total Hip machine. [gluteals, upper hamstrings, erector spinae] Hip flexion also can be performed on this machine. [hip flexors, rectus abdominus]*

Soloflex Variable Resistance

Soloflex is a single instrument that, with minor machine manipulations, can provide resistance exercise for virtually every muscle group. The resistance varies simply due to the stretching of "weight straps" during the positive phase of the lift. As the stretch of the straps increases the resistance to the muscular contraction increases. The stored energy of the stretched weightstraps provides the resistance during the eccentric phase of each exercise. Due to the "floating lever arm," caused by the flexible weightstraps, balance between limbs is easier maintained. It is easily detectable when the dominant side muscles are doing more work on the lift than those on the non-dominant side. The Soloflex bar also is adaptable to free-weights. See body weight exercises at the end of this chapter for additional Solofex exercises.

Photos used in Figure 10.26 to 10.35 were provided by Soloflex, Inc., Hawthorn Farm Industrial Park, 570 N.E. 53rd, Hillsboro, OR 97124-6494.

Figure 10.26. *Lat pull.* *[latissimus dorsi, rhomboids, biceps, brachioradialis]*

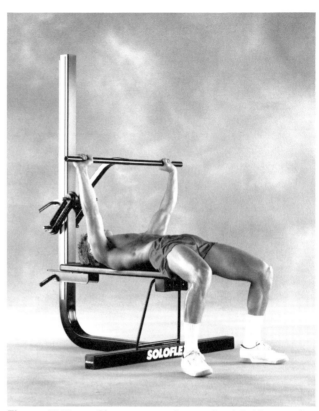

Figure 10.28. *Chest press.* *[pectorals, deltoids (anterior), triceps]*

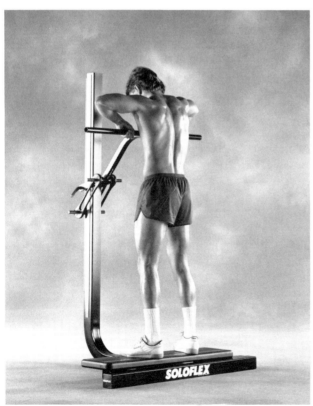

Figure 10.27. *Upright row* *[trapezius, deltoids, rhomboids, biceps, brachioradialis]*

Figure 10.29. *Shoulder (military) press. [deltoids, triceps] Can be performed facing the bar also.*

Figure 10.30. *Arm extension. [triceps]*

Figure 10.32. *Dead lift. [gluteals, quadriceps, upper hamstrings]*

Figure 10.31. *Leg extension. [quadriceps]*

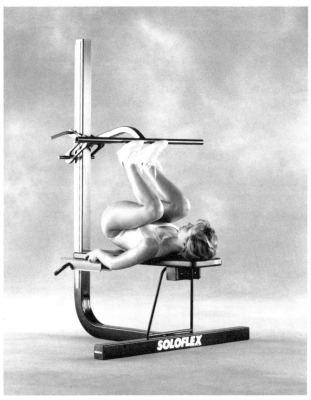

Figure 10.33. *Leg press. [quadriceps, gluteals, upper hamstrings]*

Figure 10.34. *Squat. [gluteals, quadriceps, upper hamstrings]*

Hydra-Fitness Variable Resistance

Hydra-Fitness has coined the term "omnikinetics" to describe its mechanism of variable resistance. In this method, hydraulic fluid in cylinders provide positive resistance only. The aperture size through which the fluid flows varies through the range of motion. This mechanism offers the potential for compound variable resistance. These instruments generally provide "reciprocal muscle work" in that opposing muscle groups perform concentric contractions during a single repetition. With this type of system, maintenance of muscular balance is assured. Each instrument accommodates to the force generated by the muscle during the range of motion regardless of the speed of movement. Inertia and mometum problems also are eliminated with this hydraulic resistance system.

Photos used in Figures 10.36 to 10.43 were provided by Hydra-Fitness Industries, P.O. Box 599, Belton, Texas 76513.

Figure 10.35 *Calf raises. [gastrocnemius, soleus]*

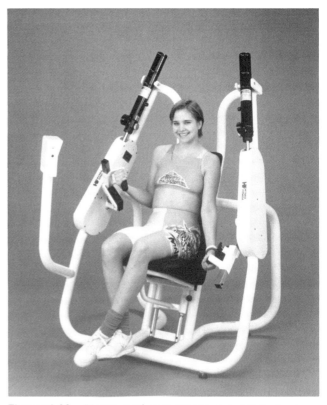

Figure 10.36. *Biceps curl and triceps extension. [curl — biceps, brachialis, brachioradialis] [extension — triceps, anconeus]*

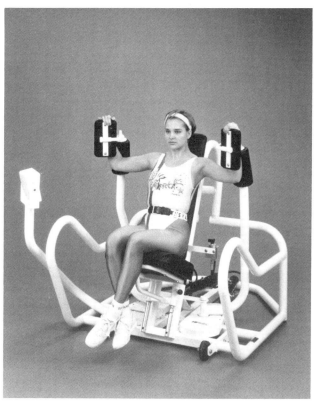

Figure 10.37. *Shoulder flexion and extension on the Butterfly machine. [flexion - pectorals, anterior, deltoid, serratus anterior] [extension - trapezius, rhomboids, latissimus dorsi]*

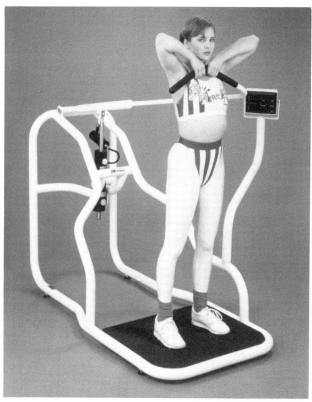

Figure 10.39. *Upright rowing and triceps extension. [rowing - trapezius, deltoids, biceps, brachioradialis] [extension - triceps, latissimus dorsi]*

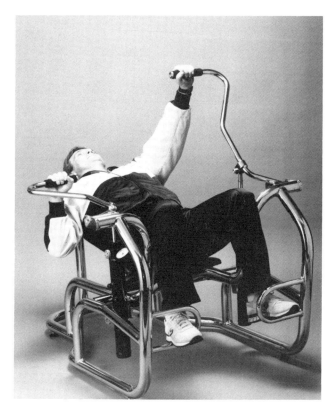

Figure 10.38. *Shoulder press and shoulder pulldown. [press - deltoids, triceps, pectorals, trapezius] [pulldown - latissimus dorsi, rhomboids, biceps, brachioradialis]*

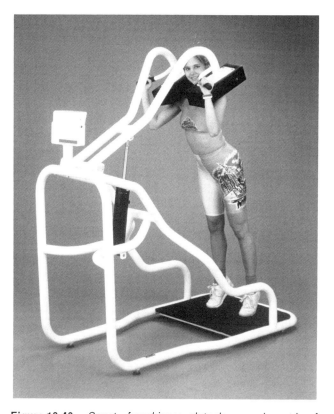

Figure 10.40. *Squat. [quadriceps, gluteals, upper hamstrings] Calf raises (plantar flexion). [gastrocnemius, soleus, peroneals]*

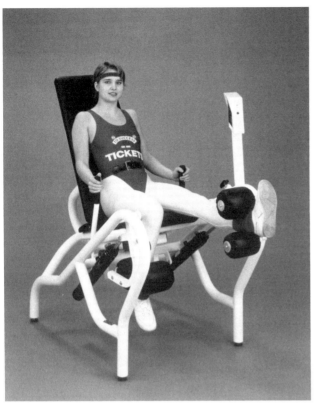

Figure 10.41. *Leg flexion and extension. [flexion - hamstrings, upper gastrocnemius] [extension - quadriceps]*

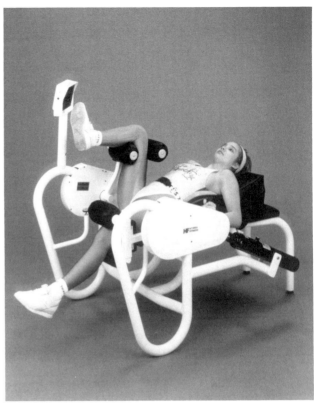

Figure 10.42. *Hip flexion/extension [flexion-upper quadriceps, erector spinae] [extension-gluteals, upper hamstrings]*

Figure 10.43. *Hydra-Fitness MAXX six station unit.*

Nautilus Variable Resistance

The Nautilus machines each have a variable shaped camp with an off-center axis (Figure 2.2). The profile of one of the early cams resembled the shell of the chambered nautilus, and thus the company name. In each of these machines the shape of the cam dictates the resistance at any specific point in the range of motion. As the pulley cable encircles a larger part of the cam, the resistance increases, and if a smaller part of the cam, the resistance decreases. Because of the cam's irregular shape, the resistance can increase and then decrease (a compound resistance change) during a single range of motion. These instruments provide resistance for both concentric and eccentric contractions.

Photos used in Figures 10.44 to 10.52 were provided by Nautilus Sports/Medical Industries, Inc., P.O. Box 160, Independence, VA 24348.

Figure 10.45. *Arm extension using Multi-Triceps machine.* *[triceps]   See Figure 2.2 for the Nautilus shoulder press.*

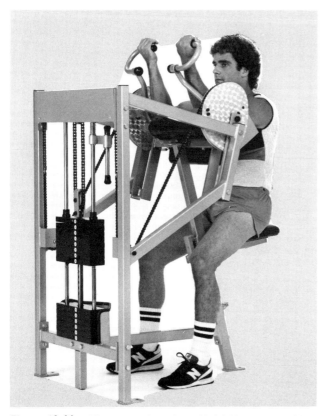

Figure 10.44. *Biceps curl using Multi-Biceps machine.* *[biceps, brachialis, forearm muscles]*

Figure 10.46. *Pullover using Women's Pullover machine.* *[latissimus dorsi, trapezius]*

Figure 10.47. Abdominal curl. [rectus abdominus, obliques]

Figure 10.49. Trunk extension using Lower Back machine. [erector spinae, gluteals]

Figure 10.48. Trunk twist on Rotary Torso machine. [obliques]

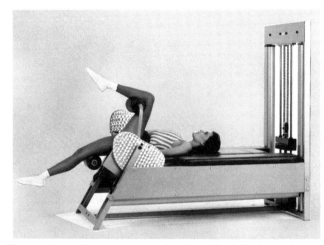

Figure 10.50. Hip extension using Duo Hip & Back machine. [gluteals, upper hamstring]

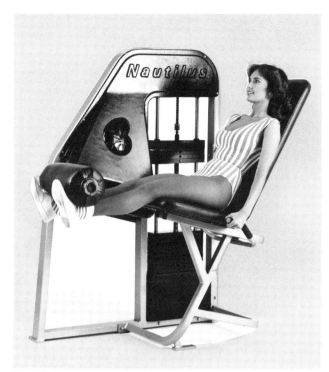

Figure 10.51. *Leg extension. [quadriceps]*

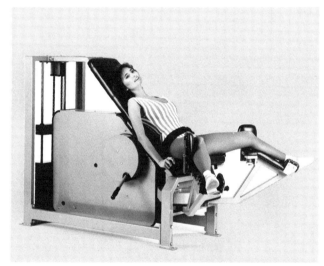

Figure 10.52. *Hip abduction and adduction. [abduction — gluteals and outer thigh muscles] [adduction — inner thigh muscles]*

Keiser Variable Resistance

These instruments provide variable resistance by trapping air using a pneumatic cylinder with piston, much like an auto engine cylinder. The amount of air in the cylinder is provided by an air compressor controlled by the user. The more air in the cylinder, the greater the initial resistance. As the lifter moves through the range of motion, the air is compressed within the cylinder, and thus the resistance gradually increases during the positive or concentric phrase of contraction. The trapped air pushes back against the cylinder piston to provide the resistance during the negative or eccentric phase. The exerciser is literally "pumping air" instead of iron with such a machine. In addition, a linkage system coupled between the cylinder and the machine handles, changes the resistance lever system during the movement, which also varies resistance. Inertia and momentum of weights are virtually eliminated in the Keiser K300 making high speed resistance training possible.

The control of the compressor provides very rapid change in the cylinder air resistance. This allows changes in loads at any phase of the exercise. For example, extra air can be introduced during the eccentric phase of contraction. Likewise, the initial air pressure can be changed between sets to allow easier load adjustment in pyramid programs. (See Chapter 11.)

Photos used in Figure 10.53 to 10.63 were provided by Keiser Sports Health Equipment, 411 S. West Avenue, Fresno, CA 93706-9952.

Figure 10.53. *Seated butterfly. [pectorals, anterior deltoid]*

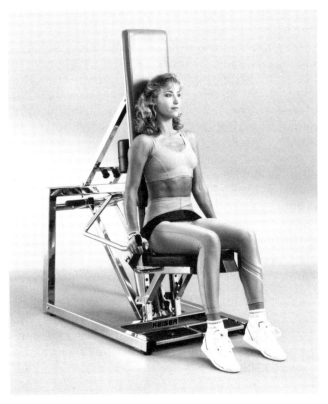

Figure 10.54. *Arm extension using the Triceps machine. [triceps]*

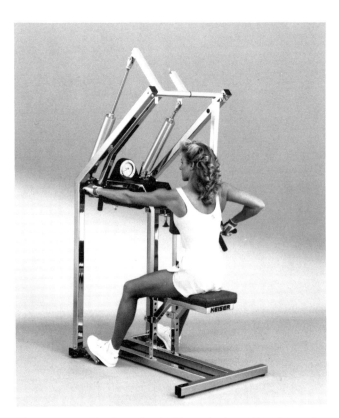

Figure 10.56. *Rowing using the Upper Back machine. [trapezius, rhomboids, biceps, brachioradialis]*

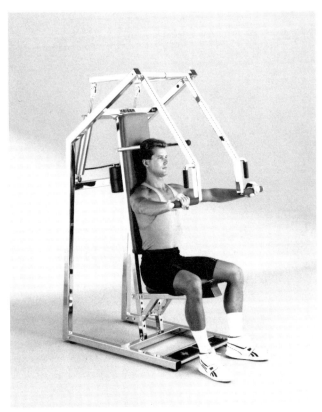

Figure 10.55. *Seated chest press. [pectorals, triceps]*

Figure 10.57. *Lat pull-down [latissimus dorsi, biceps, brachioradialis]*

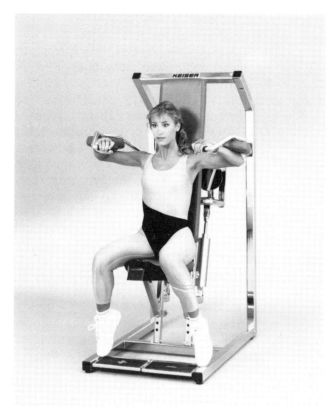

Figure 10.58. *Shoulder raises [trapezius, rhomboids, deltoids]*

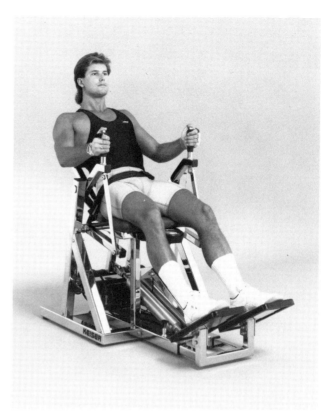

Figure 10.60. *Trunk extension on lower back machine. [erector spinae, gluteals]*

Figure 10.59. *Trunk flexion on abdominal machine. [rectus abdominis, obliques]*

Figure 10.61. *Leg press. [quadriceps, gluteals]*

95

Figure 10.62. *Standing hip abduction. [outer thigh muscles and gluteus maximus]*

Body Weight Resistance

Resistance training is possible to perform without extensive equipment. The weight of the body or weight of segments of the body can be used effectively to provide resistance for muscular contraction. Generally this type of training can produce significant strength gains early in the training program and can provide a workout for overall muscular tone. Eventually, it may be difficult to continue to "progressively overload" the muscles and strength may level off. Therefore, these exercises generally are used best in the general fitness program rather than in athletic conditioning. Early in the exercise program, the easier techniques with only a few repetitions should be performed. Progress to performing a more difficult adaptation of the exercise. As the exercise becomes easier, weights could be added to the body or the number of repetitions increased. The latter approach probably provides the best stimulus for achieving muscular tone. A weighted vest with adjustable loads is especially useful for progressively increasing the resistance in body weight exercise. It may be difficult to incorporate all muscle groups into this type of resistance program. For example, the hamstrings group are difficult to isolate using body weight exercises. Therefore, supplemental lifting may be necessary.

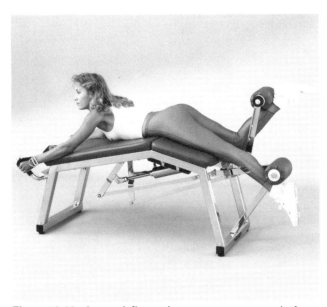

Figure 10.63. *Leg curl. [hamstrings, upper gastrocnemius]*

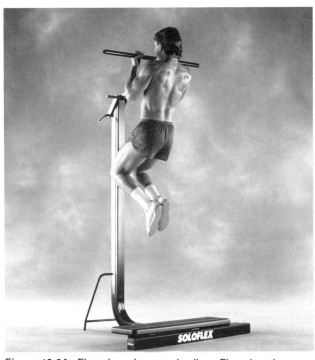

Figure 10.64. *Flexed arm hang and pull-up. Flexed armhang can be performed if the pull-up is too difficult. [underhand grip - biceps, latissiumu dorsi, pectorals, trapezius] [overhand grip - plus brachioradialis] Photo was provided by Soloflex.*

Figure 10.65. *Pull-up. Mid-grip. [emphasizes brachioradialis] Photo was provided by Soloflex.*

Figure 10.67. *Modified push-up (off the knees). Easier version of the push-up. [triceps, pectorals, deltoids]*

Figure 10.68. *Push-up. Same muscles as Figure 10.67.*

Figure 10.66. *Dip. Easier version is to hold the position. [triceps, trapezius, rhomboids, latissimus dorsi, deltoids] Photo was provided by Universal.*

Figure 10.69. *Piggy back push-up. More difficult version of the push-up. A weighted vest or other weights can be used. [triceps, pectorals, deltoids]*

Figure 10.70. *Modified sit-up. If abdominals are weak, the thighs may be grabbed to help during the up-phase of the exercise. [abdominals, obliques]*

Figure 10.71. *Incline sit-up. This exercise may be performed on a flat surface or uphill on the lawn. Twisting movement uses side muscles (obliques) more. [abdominals, obliques] Photo was provided by Universal.*

Figure 10.73. *Roman chair sit-up. Lowering torso and head below the chair increases the intensity of the exercise. [abdominals, obliques] Photo was provided by Soloflex.*

Figure 10.72. *Incline sit-up. [abdominals, obliques] Photo was provided by Soloflex.*

Figure 10.74. *Vertical sit-up. [rectus abdominus, obliques, quadriceps] Photo was provided by Soloflex.*

98

Figure 10.75. *Sit-up over a chair. [abdominals, obliques]*

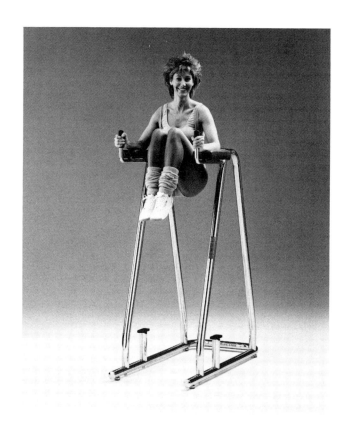

Figure 10.77. *Knee raise. Easier version is to hold knees at various heights. [lower abdominals, upper quadriceps, obliques] Photo was provided by Universal.*

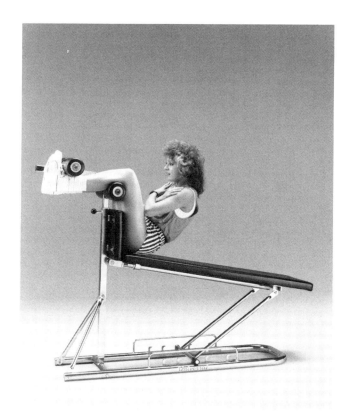

Figure 10.76. *Incline sit-up using a Crunch Bench. More difficult version of the incline sit-up. [lower abdominals, obliques] Photo was provided by Universal.*

Figure 10.78. *Body curl. Legs can be held straight throughout the movement or knees can be brought to the chest, then extended. [lower abdominals] Photo was provided by Soloflex.*

99

Figure 10.79A. *Knee lift. From extended position, bend knees slightly and raise feet off the ground; bring knees to chest and return to starting position. Easier version is to perform movement with one leg at a time. [quadriceps, lower abdominals]*

Figure 10.79B. *Knee lift. More difficult version is to keep both heels off the floor during the exercise. Always keep back flat against the floor. If this is not possible, do not perform the difficult version.*

Figure 10.80. *Heel raises off a ledge. An easier version is to perform this exercise off the floor. [gastrocnemius, soleus]*

1. Resistance Exercises Using Muscles
of the
ARMS and SHOULDERS

MUSCLES

Exercises & Figures	BICEPS & BRACHIALIS	BRACHIO-RADIALIS	TRICEPS	FOREARM MUSCLES	DELTOIDS			
Arm Curl 10.2, 10.3, 10.11, 10.17A, 10.36, 10.44	X	X		X				
Bent-Over Row 10.7, 10.17, 10.56	X	X						
Upright Row 10.8, 10.27, 10.39	X	X			X			
Chest Press 10.4, 10.12, 10.13, 10.28, 10.55			X		X			
Shoulder Press 10.5, 10.6, 10.14, 10.29, 10.38			X		X			
Arm Extension 10.17A, 10.30, 10.39, 10.45			X					
Shoulder Flexion 10.15, 10.37. 10.53					X			
Pull-Up 10.58, 10.64, 10.65	X	X		X				
Push-Up 10.67, 10.68, 10.69			X		X			
Dip 10.66			X		X			

2. Resistance Exercises Using Muscles
of the
CHEST and BACK

MUSCLES

Exercises & Figures	PECTORALS	ANTERIOR SERRATUS	TRAPEZIUS	RHOMBOIDS	LATISSIMUS DORSI	ERECTOR SPINAE		
Chest Press 10.4, 10.12, 10.13, 10.28, 10.55	X							
Shoulder Press 10.5, 10.6, 10.14, 10.29, 10.38			X					
Bent-Over Row 10.7, 10.17, 10.56			X	X	X			
Upright Row 10.8, 10.27, 10.39			X					
Shoulder Raises 10.58			X	X				
Butterfly 10.15, 10.37, 10.53	X	X						
Lat Pulldown 10.16, 10.26, 10.57				X	X			
Pullover 10.46			X		X			
Pull-Up 10.58, 10,74			X		X			
Push-Up 10.60, 10.61, 10.62	X							
Dip 10.59			X	X	X			
Back Extension 10.19, 10.42, 10.49						X		

3. Resistance Exercises Using Muscles
of the
MIDDLE BODY

MUSCLES

Exercises & Figures	GLUTEALS	UPPER HAMSTRINGS	ABDOMINALS	OBLIQUES	HIP FLEXORS	UPPER QUADRICEPS	ERECTOR SPINAE	
Leg Squat 10.9, 10.21, 10.34, 10.40	X	X						
Trunk Extension 10.19, 10.42, 10.49, 10.60	X						X	
Leg Press 10.20, 10.33, 10.61	X	X						
Hip Extension 10.24, 10.42, 10.50	X	X					X	
Hip Abduction 10.52, 10.62	X					X		
Hip Adduction 10.25, 10.52	X					X		
Dead Lift 10.32	X	X						
Trunk Flexion 10.24, 10.42, 10.59			X	X	X			
Abdominal Curl 10.47			X	X				
Truck Twist 10.48				X				
Sit-Up 10.70, 10.71, 10.72, 10.73, 10.74, 10.75, 10.76			X	X	X	X		
Knee Raise 10.77, 10.79			X	X	X	X		
Body Curl 10.78			X		X			

4. Resistance Exercises Using Muscles
of the
LEGS

MUSCLES

Exercises & Figures	QUADRICEPS	HAMSTRINGS	GASTROC-NEMIUS	SOLEUS	PERONEALS			
Leg Squat 10.9, 10.21, 10.34, 10.40	X							
Heel Raise 10.10, 10.35, 10.40, 10.80			X	X	X			
Leg Press 10.20, 10.33, 10.61	X							
Leg Extension 10.22, 10.31, 10.41, 10.51	X							
Leg Flexion 10.23, 10.41, 10.63		X	X					
Dead Lift 10.32	X							
Hip Flexion 10.42	X							
Hip Extension 10.24, 10.42, 9.50		X						
Knee Raises 10.77, 10.79	X							

RESISTANCE TRAINING FOR SPECIFIC ACTIVITIES

The general guidelines discussed in previous chapters can be helpful in designing an effective resistance program. Most individuals will have a primary goal they wish to achieve with the exercise program. This goal may change during different times of the year or as the individual grows older. The primary purpose of the resistance program can be classified into two general areas: 1. athletic competition, training for maximal strength and power gains. 2. cardiovascular fitness and muscular tone, training for general muscular strength and fitness. In this chapter, the specifics of resistance programs will be outlined. A minimum of 10 minutes of stretching exercises should be performed before and after each exercise period in all resistance programs. (See Chapter 5.)

MUSCULAR STRENGTH AND POWER

The program presented is an adaptation of the University of Nebraska method developed by Boyd Epley. In general, heavy loads and few repetitions are used. Also part of this system is "pyramiding" in which loads are progressively increased during the exercise period. Loads also are progressively increased or "pyramided" over a given time period in the program. The training regimen uses "cycling" in which the exercise intensity is varied workout to workout and over set time periods to avoid staleness and training plateaus. Each major muscle group is exercised two times per week, once heavy and once medium. At least two days rest is taken between sessions using the same muscle groups. The chest and legs are exercised on Monday (heavy) and Thursday (medium), and the back, shoulders, and arms on Tuesday (heavy) and Friday (medium).

A simpler program can be performed by young athletes or athletes participating in sports which do not necessarily require maximal strength efforts. In this simpler system three sets of six repetitions (6RM) are used for each muscle group and all body parts three times per week (alternate days). It is important that the muscles associated with the sport be emphasized and muscular balance maintained. This program is very effective in producing strength and hypertrophy gains in previously untrained young adults.

A program similar in intensity to the Epley system can be used for any sport in which maximal muscular strength and power are required. Such intense training generally is reserved for high-level competitive athletics and is especially effective in power sports such as football, basketball, volleyball, and track and field. This high intensity program is not necessary nor recommended for the recreational athlete.

The cycling "phases" progress from light to maximum intensity:

Phase 1
 10 reps
 3 sets
 1st set 65% of 1 RM
 2nd set 70%
 3rd set 75%
 1-2 minutes between exercises
 1-2 week duration

Phase 2
 8 reps
 4 sets
 1st set 65%
 2nd set 70%
 3rd set 75%
 4th set 75%
 2 minutes between exercises
 1-2 week duration
 reduce loads by 5% on medium days
 e.g., 1st set = 60% of 1 RM

Phase 3
 6 reps
 4 sets
 1st set 65%
 2nd set 75%
 3rd set 75%
 4th set 80%
 2 minutes rest between exercises
 1 week duration
 reduce loads by 5% on medium days

Phase 4
  10, 8, 4, 3 reps
  4 sets
  10 reps at 50%
  8 reps at 60%
  4 reps at 80%
  3 reps at 85%
  2 minutes rest between exercises
  1 week duration
  reduce loads by 5% on medium days

  Start again at Phase 1.

"Power training" can be incorporated into this strength regimen by using power drills on non-lifting days (Wednesday and weekends) or before the strength routine on leg days (Monday and Thursday). Power drills might include high knees, ankle flips, stair runs, hopping, jumping, plyometrics. (See *Husker Power* reference in Suggested Readings list.)

Power resistance training also can be performed on a fifth workout day in which lighter loads and faster contractions are used. Loads of about 40-60% can be used with lifts made as rapidly as possible. Such a program is feasible only when non-weight resistance equipment is available. Momentum caused by rapidly lifting free-weights and weight stacks can reduce the resistance on the muscle and increase the risk of injury. Some form of power training should be incorporated into the resistance program whether in-season or off-season.

Maintenance

Once strength and power are gained, they are fairly easy to retain. Maintenance training during the season can include using the medium day only, each muscular group used one day per week. As an alternative, one exercise can be performed for each muscle group twice a week (heavy and medium) at intensities equivalent to phase 3 of the cycle.

Exercises

Example exercises are given. Alternatives which affect similar muscular groups can be used. Illustrations in Chapter 10 can be used for descriptions of the exercises and to determine alternative exercises depending on the equipment available. Additional exercises can be selected if the sport demands greater training of specific muscle groups. The sequence of exercises are arranged so that the same muscle group is not used in successive exercises. Appendix A contains workout records for logging daily resistance training workouts.

Monday (heavy) and Thursday (medium)
  Chest and Legs
1. Bench Press
2. Squat
3. Incline Press or Chest Butterfly
4. Leg Curl
5. Heel Raise
6. Leg Extension or Leg Press
7. Ankle Flexion
8. Hip Extension and Flexion

Tuesday (heavy) and Friday (medium)
  Arms, Shoulders, Back
1. Arm Curl
2. Shoulder Press
3. Lat Pulldown
4. Arm Extension
5. Upright Row
6. Incline Shoulder Press
7. Bent-over Row
8. Shoulder Shrug

Monday-Friday (4 times/week)
  Abdominal-Trunk
  One set of 25 each
1. Incline Sit-Up or Roman-Chair Sit-Up
2. Abdominal Curl on machine
3. Knee Raise or Knee Lift

Appendices B and C contain strength and girth evaluations.

CARDIOVASCULAR FITNESS AND MUSCULAR TONE

Resistance training for general fitness is somewhat different in intensity than a program designed to maximize strength and power. Cardiovascular fitness is not developed using heavy resistances. Rather, lighter loads are used and the number of repetitions increased. In addition, the time between exercises is reduced to 15 seconds and a sequence of exercises is performed in close succession. The goal of such a routine is to maintain heart rate and oxygen consumption within a target zone necessary to elicit cardiovascular or aerobic training. The exercise intensity should be maintained continuously for 30-45 minutes. (See Table 11.1).

Circuit Resistance Training

A circuit resistance training (CRT) program is the best type of resistance exercise system for producing the desired aerobic effect. Such a routine will not produce maximal strength and bulk gains. But strength gains can be significant and the continuous, moderate exercise promotes beneficial changes in body

Table 11.1. *Characteristics of Cardiovascular Exercise Training*
1. Moderate Intensity: 60% maximal oxygen consumption or 75% maximal heart rate (140-160 beats per min)
2. Prolonged: At least 30 minutes of continuous activity
3. Continuous: Non-stop activity
4. Frequent: 3-4 times per week, alternate days
5. Large muscle groups: Total body activity, especially the legs
6. Extended: At least one year program duration
Example activities: jogging, brisk walking, swimming, level cycling, skilled rope jumping, hiking, rowing, cross country skiing, some types of aerobic rhythms

composition and cardiovascular fitness. Likewise, improvements in aerobic capacity will not be maximal. But gains can be expected and maintenance of aerobic fitness is possible with the CRT routines. Multistation resistance systems, such as the one illustrated in Figure 11.1, are ideal for CRT programs.

This type of program is recommended for individuals interested in aerobic fitness. It is especially beneficial for the recreational athlete who seeks general fitness and wishes to improve tennis, racketball, basketball, jogging, etc. performance. Individuals interested in optimal cardiovascular fitness must use other aerobic

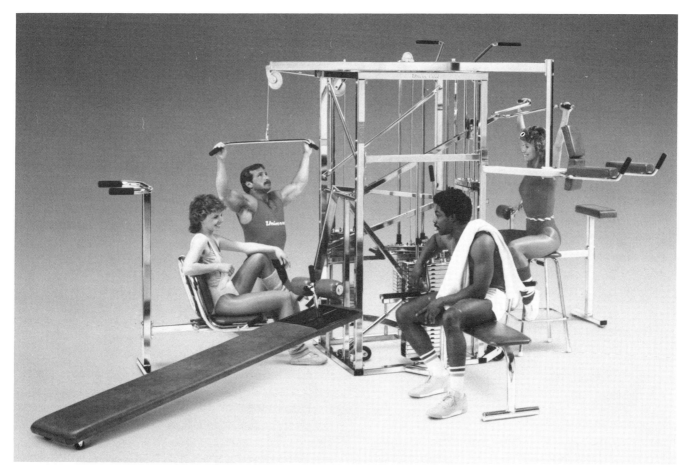

Figure 11.1.   *Universal Multistation System. Photo was provided by Universal, P.O. Box 1270, Cedar Rapids, IA 52406.*

activities as the primary exercise. However, CRT can supplement and serve as a short-term substitute for the regular aerobic program. Aerobic exercisers may find the CRT routine a welcome diversion.

Like heavy resistance training, CRT can be performed on alternate days. A Monday, Wednesday, Friday Program is outlined here, but a two day per week program is best in which the CRT is alternated with regular aerobic exercise, and the total conditioning program is five items per week. For example, jogging or aerobics is performed on Monday, Wednesday, and Friday and the CRT workout on Tuesday and Thursday.

Inserting an aerobic vehicle in the CRT routine can enhance the cardiovascular component of the workout and provide diversity. Aerobic "ergometers" are instruments which provide a means of performing aerobic exercise. They are relatively inexpensive and can provide a warm-up and cool down exercise as well as be included in the CRT routine. Such exercise should be performed for 3-5 minutes to allow the cardiovascular system to adapt to the exercise.

A cycle ergometer is an excellent addition to the CRT routine (Figure 11.2). The low-sit cycle provides a comfortable exercise position, and this position enhances venous return during the exercise (Figure 11.3). Low-sit cycling also is an excellent exercise to use during recovery from the workout. The load on cycles is easily adjustable, and the exercise easy to learn even for populations with low fitness and motor skills. A treadmill also can be used in the CRT routine (Figure 11.4). This machine is especially useful for individuals who enjoy walking activities. This type of exercise is particularly beneficial for the recreational athlete who relies on leg fitness in the sport. For more total body muscular involvement, the rowing ergometer and the cross-country skiier can be used. In the rower, the upper body musculature produces a substantial portion of effort (Figure 11.5). This activity is fairly easy to learn and offers a diverse form of physical activity. It is especially useful for individuals who already have some degree of physical fitness. The skiing simulator involves a total body activity with less jarring on the joints than jogging (Figure 11.6). This instrument requires some practice to become proficient at the activity. It is especially useful in weight loss programs because the skiing exercise causes the use of more calories than most activities. Stair climbing is another exercise which involves a large portion of the body's musculature. Figure 11.7 illustrates a stair climbing simulation, sort of a "stair treadmill." The hand railings can be used to provide stability in untrained or elderly individuals.

Figure 11.2. *Universal AerobiCycle. Photo was provided by Universal Gym Equipment Inc., P.O. Box 1270, Cedar Rapids, IA 52406.*

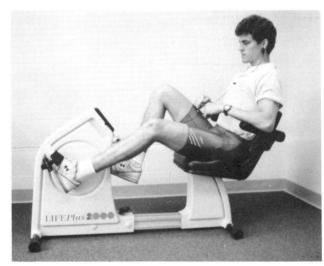

Figure 11.3. *LIFEPlus 2000 low-sit cycle. Photo was provided by LIFEPlus, Inc., 3770 Plaza Drive, Suite 1, Ann Arbor, MI 48108-1654.*

Figure 11.4. *Universal Tredex motorized treadmill. Photo was provided by Universal Gym Equipment, Inc.*

Figure 11.6. *Nordic Track Achiever ski simulator. Photo was provided by Nordic Track, 141 Jonathan Boulevard North, Chaska, MN 55318-2342.*

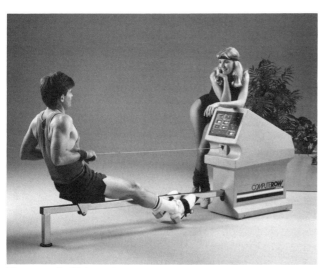

Figure 11.5. *Universal ComputeRow rowing machine. Photo was provided by Universal Gym Equipment, Inc.*

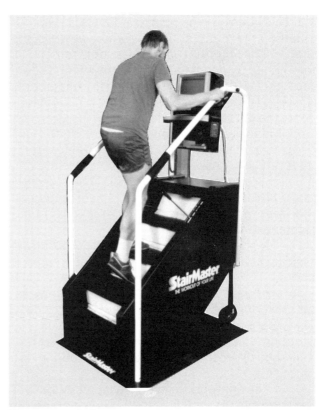

Figure 11.7. *Stairmaster 6000. Photo was provided by Randal Sports/Medical Products, Inc., 12421 Willows Road, N.E., Suite 100, Kirkland, WA 98034.*

These aerobic ergometers also can serve as the primary exercise in the cardiovascular fitness program. The exercise should be performed at a moderate intensity for 30 to 45 minutes on alternate days. The exercise intensity should be low for the initial five minutes (warm-up) and the final five minutes (cool-down) of the exercise bout.

Heart Rate Monitoring

An important consideration of any exercise program is the intensity of the work, which is accurately indicated by the heart rate. The rate which the heart is beating can be determined by palpating the area over the heart or over any artery. Naturally some areas provide easier palpation than others. Sites typically used include the lower left side of the chest at about the fifth rib, the radial artery in the wrist on the thumb side, and the carotid artery of the neck. Some researchers have determined that carotid artery palpation at the neck can reflexly slow the heart rate. Therefore, other sites should be attempted, and if the carotid is used, only very light fingertip pressure should be applied. Locate the pulse with the index and middle fingertips, and count the number of beats for a six second time period exactly. Start counting with the number "1" if using a sweep second hand watch. Begin with "0" if starting the count and a stopwatch at the same time. The number of beats per minute is determined by adding a "0" to the six second count (multiply by 10). Practice counting the heart beats at rest. To determine the "exercise heart rate," locate the pulse just prior to stopping the exercise. Stop and immediately count the number of beats for six seconds. Add a "0" and this is the exercise heart rate in beats per minute (bpm). Be sure and maintain a steady exercise pace prior to taking the heart rate. For example, lifting rapidly at the end of a work-out will cause an overestimation of the normal exercise heart rate.

A variety of new automatic heart rate devices, such as finger and ear meters, are on the market. These seem to provide a reasonably accurate heart rate if the individual is motionless, but most are very sensitive to movement. These devices do offer an alternative to palpation and counting. They also allow the exerciser to continuously monitor the heart rate during the exercise.

The appropriate exercise intensity for CRT and aerobic exercise can be determined by estimating the maximal heart rate (HR max) and then calculating the target exercise heart rate (EHR) as 75% of maximal:

$$\text{HR max} = 220 - \text{age (years)}$$
$$\text{EHR} = \text{HR max} \times 0.75$$
$$\text{e.g., HR max} = 220 - 40 \text{ years} = 180 \text{ bpm}$$
$$\text{EHR} = 180 \times 0.75 = 135 \text{ bpm}$$

Use a range of about 5 bpm around the target heart rate; in the example, the EHR range would be 130-140 bpm. The exercise should be performed within this heart rate range at the pace which feels most comfortable and produces a comfortable breathing pattern.

CRT Exercises

Generally, free-weights are not appropriate for CRT. Machines which allow rapid changes in the loads are best because delays between exercises can lessen the potential cardiovascular effect.

The program described below is for three times per week using lighter weights and more repetitions than the heavy resistance program designed for athletes. For each exercise, 12-15 repetitions are performed using loads of 40 to 50% of 1RM. It is not necessary or desirable to lift to failure in this type of training. To determine the 40-50% resistance, simply use a load which causes near fatigue after 18-20 repetitions. If no aerobic mode is used, a 15 second rest is taken between each resistance exercise. After completion of the total sequence (1-13), the routine is repeated omitting #1 and #2. After 2 cycles, the session is ended with cool down (#15) and stretching (#16). The total routine is designed to be completed in 45-50 minutes.

Monday, Wednesday, Friday or
Tuesday, Thursday, Saturday

1. stretching exercises - 6 minutes - no rest period
2. warm-up on cycle - 4 minutes
3. chest press or shoulder press
4. lat pull or pull-up - no rest period
5. ski ergometer - 3 minutes
6. incline sit-ups or abdominal curl
7. leg press or squat - no rest period
8. treadmill walk - 3 minutes
9. trunk extension
10. leg curl
11. knee raise or knee lift
12. heel raise - no rest period
13. rowing ergometer - 3 minutes
14. repeat stations 3 through 13
15. cool down on low-sit cycle - 5 minutes
16. stretching exercises - 6 minutes

Other resistance exercises and other modes of aerobic ergometers can be used in the CRT routine. A single aerobic ergometer can be used in each three minute aerobic session during the routine, but a variety may help keep the routine more enjoyable. It is important to utilize all muscle groups. More upper body resistance exercises can be substituted for the lower body exercises if jogging, aerobics, skiing, or other leg activities are the primary exercise modes in the aerobic program. Appendix A contains workout records for logging CRT training bouts.

As an alternative to the described CRT program, the ergometers can be used during the "rest period" itself. Following each resistance exercise, the aerobic ergometer is used for a 30 to 60 second recovery period. In this way, the heart rate remains continuously elevated, and no real rest is taken during the exercise session. This method is often called "super circuit resistance training."

SUGGESTED READINGS

1. Epley, B. *Husker Power.* Lincoln, NE: Boyd Epley, 1983.
2. Gettman, L.R., and M.L. Pollock. Circuit weight training: a critical review of its physiological benefits. *The Physician and Sports Medicine* 9(1): 44-60, Jan., 1981.
3. Hurley, B.F. and P.F. Kokkinos. Effects of weight training on risk factors for coronary artery disease. *Sports Medicine* 4: 231-238, 1987.
4. Kraemer, W.J. and S.J. Fleck. Resistance training: exercise prescription (Part 4). *Physician and Sportsmedicine* 16:69-81, June, 1988.
5. Thomas, T.R. and C.J. Zebas. *Scientific Exercise Training.* Dubuque: Kendall/Hunt, 1987.

112

APPENDICES

WORKOUT RECORDS and FITNESS EVALUATIONS

The following appendices contain workout records and evaluation methods to help in monitoring your progress.

The fitness charts are intended to be completed at periodic intervals (about one month) so that a program can be adjusted to meet your specific goals.

A. **RESISTANCE TRAINING WORKOUT RECORDS**
   1. **STRENGTH PROGRAM**
   2. **CIRCUIT RESISTANCE TRAINING PROGRAM (CRT)**

B. **STRENGTH ASSESSMENT**

C. **GIRTH ASSESSMENT**

D. **BODY FAT ASSESSMENT**

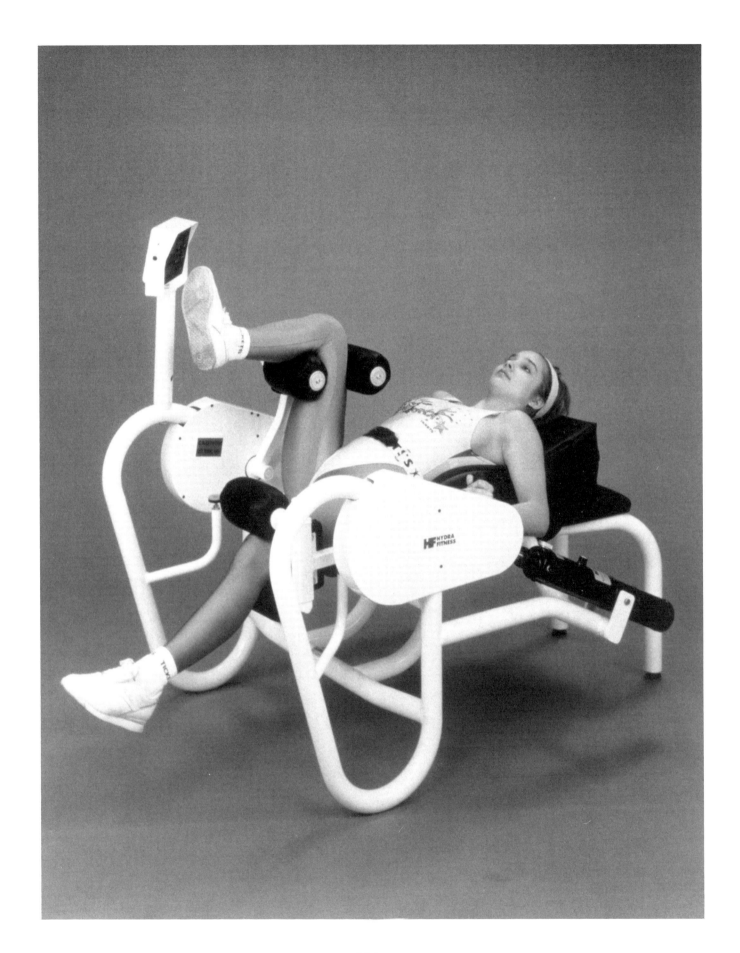

114

RESISTANCE TRAINING
WORKOUT RECORDS

1.) Strength Program

Name _____

Date	Exercise	Load Lbs.	Load % of 1 RM	Sets	Body Weight	Total Work-out Time

Strength Program

Name _____

Date	Exercise	Load Lbs.	Load % of 1 RM	Sets	Body Weight	Total Work-out Time

Strength Program

Name _____

Date	Exercise	Load Lbs.	Load % of 1 RM	Sets	Body Weight	Total Work-out Time

Strength Program

Name _____

Date	Exercise	Load Lbs.	Load % of 1 RM	Sets	Body Weight	Total Work-out Time

2.) Circuit Resistance Training Program
(CRT)

Name _____

Date	Exercise	Load % of 1 RM	Exercise Heart Rate	Aerobic Mode	Body Weight	Total Work-out Time

Circuit Resistance Training Program
(CRT)

Name _____

Date	Exercise	Load % of 1 RM	Exercise Heart Rate	Aerobic Mode	Body Weight	Total Work-out Time

Circuit Resistance Training Program
(CRT)

Name _____

Date	Exercise	Load % of 1 RM	Exercise Heart Rate	Aerobic Mode	Body Weight	Total Work-out Time

Circuit Resistance Training Program
(CRT)

Name _____

Date	Exercise	Load % of 1 RM	Exercise Heart Rate	Aerobic Mode	Body Weight	Total Work- out Time

STRENGTH ASSESSMENT

PUSH-UPS

Perform the maximum number of push-ups possible, up to 40. The chest must touch the ground and the arm fully enxtend on each repetition (Figure 10.61). No rest should be taken between repetitions. Record the results on page 127.

Table B.1. *Scoring for the Push-up Test*				
NUMBER OF PUSH-UPS				
Strength Category	Men under 35	Men over 35	Women under 35	Women over 35
High	>35	>20	>25	>15
Average (Adequate)	15-35	10-20	10-25	5-15
Low	5-14	2-9	2-9	1-4

SIT-UPS

Perform the maximum number of sit-ups possible, up to 75. The feet are not supported. The head should go beyond the upright position in the up phase and touch the floor on the down phase. No rest should be taken between repetitions. Record the results on page 127.

Table B.2. *Scoring for the Sit-up Test*				
NUMBER OF SIT-UPS				
Strength Category	Men under 35	Men over 35	Women under 35	Women over 35
High	>75	>50	>50	>30
Average (Adequate)	30-75	20-50	25-50	15-30
Low	15-29	10-19	10-24	5-14

ONE-REPETITION MAXIMUM

A more accurate method of assessing strength requires the use of barbells or a weight machine. Before the test, stretching the muscle to be used is important, and warming up with light lifting is beneficial. The test requires that the individual progress to lifting as much weight as possible, i.e., a one repetition maximum (1 RM). The maximum lift should be made within three trials to avoid the effects of fatigue. Free-weights or weight machines can be used. Determination of the 1 RM is made on four different lifts: overhead press, chest press, biceps curl, and leg press. These four lifts give an accurate indication of overall body strength. Allow at least two minutes of recovery between each maximal attempt.

Table B.4. *Scoring for One Repetition Maximum Strength Tests*

| Lift | STRENGTH CATEGORY | | | | | |
| | High | | Average | | Low | |
	Men	Women	Men	Women	Men	Women
Shoulder Press	100*	66*	66	45	50	35
Bench Press	150	100	100	70	75	50
Arm Curl	75	50	50	35	40	25
Leg Press	250	200	200	150	150	100
TOTAL (%)	575	416	416	300	315	210

* All scores are % of body weight

Reprinted with permission from T.R. Thomas and C.J. Zebas. *Scientific Exercise Training.* Copyright © 1987 by Kendall/Hunt Publishing Co.

Not all individuals should attempt to achieve a 1 RM. Very sedentary, elderly, very young, or diseased individuals should estimate a 1RM using Table B.5. In this procedure, the lifter determines the maximal amount of resistance which corresponds to the number of repetitions in the table. For example, an untrained young woman (weight=50 kg) can lift 20 kg 10 times on the bench press (a maximal effort). The 1 RM is estimated by: 20 kg/0.8=25 kg. According to Table B.4., the individual is low in strength for this muscle group. This method provides an estimate only, but does allow the determination of the starting point in the resistance program and a reasonable evaluation of progress made.

Table B.5. *Estimation of 1RM from Submaximal Lifts (# of Reps)*

Lift	Untrained	Trained*
Shoulder Press	10	10
Bench Press	10	12
Arm Curl	8	10
Leg Press	14	20

* Previous resistance training at least 3 times per week. To estimate 1RM: Determine the maximal load which can be lifted the designated number of repetitions. This load corresponds to 80% maximum. Thus, 1 RM load=80%load/0.8. Table derived from the data of W.K. Hoeger et al. *J. Appl. Sport Sci. Research.* 4(2):47-54, 1990.

Strength Changes
Record Sheet

Name_____ Sex _____ Date_____

PUSH-UPS AND SIT-UPS

Test	1st test	2nd test	3rd test
Number of Push-ups	_____	_____	_____
Strength Category	_____	_____	_____
Number of Sit-ups	_____	_____	_____
Strength Category	_____	_____	_____

ONE REPETITION MAXIMUM

	1st test	2nd test	3rd test
Date	_____	_____	_____
Body Weight	_____	_____	_____

Lift	Wt Lifted	% BW	Wt Lifted	% BW	Wt Lifted	% BW
Overhead Press	_____	____	_____	____	_____	____
Chest Press	_____	____	_____	____	_____	____
Biceps Curl	_____	____	_____	____	_____	____
Leg Press	_____	____	_____	____	_____	____
Total	_____	____	_____	____	_____	____

$$\% \text{ BW} = \text{Percent of body weight} = \frac{\text{Wt Lifted}}{\text{Body Weight}} \times 100$$

GIRTH ASSESSMENT

Changes in muscular size are associated with changes in muscular strength. Any limb or body segment can be used to measure girth changes caused by a resistance training program. It is important to measure the girth at the same spot each time. Any tape measure can be used, but a constant tension steel tape is most accurate. The tape must be held straight around the body part. Total body girth can be monitored using four girth measurements:

Upper Arm: With the arm hanging at the side, measure halfway between the top of the armpit and the bend at the elbow. The fully flexed arm also can be used, and the measurement made at the maximal girth of the biceps. Repeat on the opposite limb.

Thigh: With the weight on the opposite leg, measure the distance around the upper leg halfway between the crotch and the top of the knee, a point in the middle of the thigh. Repeat on the opposite leg.

Chest: In a standing position, with the chest muscles relaxed, measure across the nipples.

Abdomen: Again in a standing position, measure around the stomach across the navel. Record the results on the next page.

Girth Record Sheet

Name_____

Date_____

Body Weight _____

SIZE (INCHES)

	1st test	2nd test	Differences (Test 2 − Test 1)	3rd test	Differences (Test 3 − Test 1)
Upper Arm right	_____	_____	_____	_____	_____
left	_____	_____	_____	_____	_____
Upper Leg right	_____	_____	_____	_____	_____
left	_____	_____	_____	_____	_____
Chest	_____	_____	_____	_____	_____
Abdomen	_____	_____	_____	_____	_____
Net Gain (Loss)			_____		_____

BODY FAT ASSESSMENT

D

The most accurate method of assessing body fat is by hydrostatic weighing with directly measured lung volume (Chapter 7). If possible, an individual should have body fat and optimal weight estimated using hydrostatic weighing. Skinfold measurements can provide a reasonable estimate of body composition if great care is taken to measure at the precise anatomical location and if supervised practice in the use of the skinfold caliper is performed. One of the simplest skinfold techniques for men or women involves the measurement of skinfolds at three sites on the dominant side of the body. These measurements can be made with any skinfold caliper (Figure D.1 and D.2). Proper measurement locations are illustrated in Figures D.3 and D.4.

The sum of the three skinfolds is converted to % fat in Table D.1 and D.2. Record the results on the record sheet on page 139.

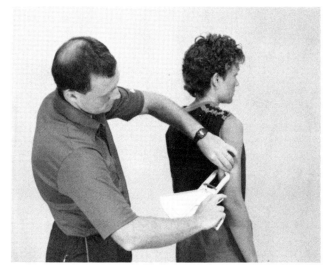

Figure D.1. *Skinfold measurement with inexpensive Slim Guide caliper.*

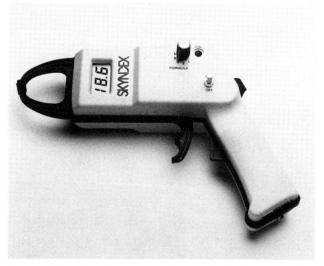

Figure D.2. *The Skyndex electronic body fat calculator. This instrument automatically calculates percent fat from the sum of the skinfolds. Photo was provided by Cramer Products, Inc., P.O. Box 1001, Gardner, KS 66030.*

The amount of body fat necessary for optimal health and fitness is unknown. However, the "average values" for any age group are probably higher than idea! For example, and estimate of ideal % fat for a young man and woman would be 10 and 18%, respectively, values which are slightly below the average for the college age group (Table D.3). These "ideal" estimates can be used to age 30 and then higher estimates are probably more appropriate.

The loss of body weight through exercise should be primarily from fat stores. To insure this, the weight loss program must involve routine aerobic activity or circuit resistance training which utilize body fat. Remember, the calculations provide only an estimate of body composition. This procedure can be used only to predict a rough estimate of an appropriate body weight goal.

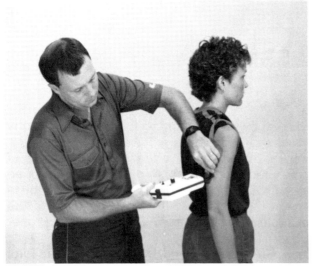

Figure D.3a. *Triceps skinfold for women. Vertical fold midway between the tip of the shoulder bone and the tip of the elbow.*

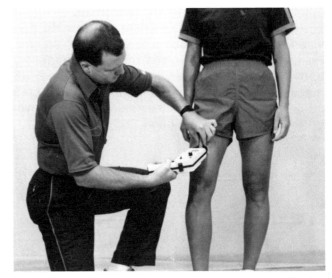

Figure D.3c. *Thigh skinfold for women. Vertical fold in the middle of the thigh.*

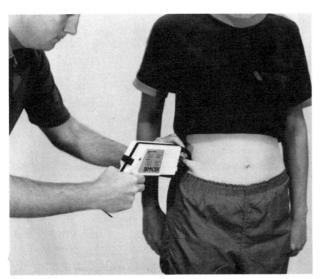

Figure D.3b. *Suprailium skinfold for women. Horizontal fold over the hip bone.*

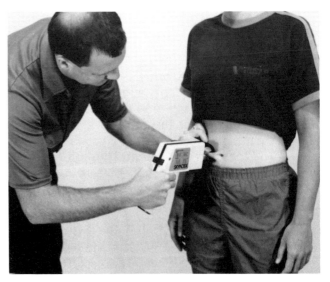

Figure D.3d. *The Skyndex System I requires the measurement of a fourth skinfold. Abdominal skinfold for women. Horizontal fold just next to the navel.*

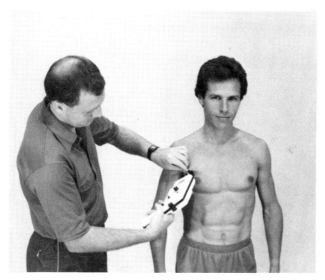

Figure D.4a. *Chest skinfold for men. Diagonal fold between the nipple and arm pit.*

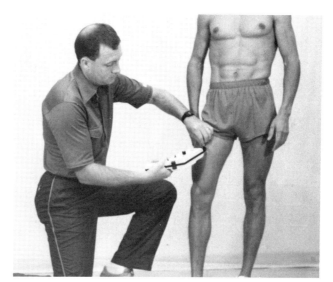

Figure D.4c. *Thigh skinfold for men. Vertical fold in the middle of the thigh.*

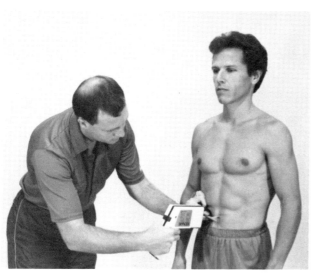

Figure D.4b. *Abdominal skinfold for men. Horizontal fold just next to the navel.*

135

Table D.1. *Female Percent Body Fat Conversion from the Sum of Three Skinfolds.*

Sum of 3 Skinfolds (mm)	18-22	23-27	28-32	33-37	38-42	43-47	48-52	53-57	58-62	Sum of 3 Skinfolds (mm)	18-22	23-27	28-32	33-37	38-42	43-47	48-52	53-57	58-62
16	7.8	8.1	8.4	8.7	8.9	9.2	9.5	9.8	10.1	72	27.3	27.6	27.9	28.3	28.6	28.9	29.2	29.6	29.9
18	8.5	8.8	9.1	9.4	9.7	10.0	10.3	10.6	10.9	74	27.9	28.2	28.6	28.9	29.2	29.5	29.8	30.2	30.5
20	9.3	9.6	9.9	10.2	10.5	10.8	11.1	11.4	11.7	76	28.5	28.8	29.2	29.5	29.8	30.1	30.4	30.8	31.1
22	10.1	10.4	10.7	11.0	11.3	11.6	11.9	12.2	12.5	78	29.1	29.4	29.7	30.1	30.4	30.7	31.0	31.4	31.7
24	10.8	11.1	11.4	11.7	12.0	12.3	12.6	12.9	13.2	80	29.7	30.0	30.3	30.7	31.0	31.3	31.6	32.0	32.3
26	11.6	11.9	12.2	12.5	12.8	13.1	13.4	13.7	14.0	82	30.3	30.6	30.9	31.2	31.6	31.9	32.2	32.5	32.9
28	12.3	12.6	12.9	13.2	13.5	13.8	14.2	14.5	14.8	84	30.8	31.2	31.5	31.8	32.1	32.5	32.8	33.1	33.4
30	13.1	13.4	13.7	14.0	14.3	14.6	14.9	15.2	15.5	86	31.4	31.7	32.0	32.4	32.7	33.0	33.4	33.7	34.0
32	13.8	14.1	14.4	14.7	15.0	15.3	15.6	15.9	16.3	88	32.0	32.3	32.6	32.9	33.3	33.6	33.9	34.2	34.6
34	14.6	14.9	15.2	15.5	15.8	16.1	16.4	16.7	17.0	90	32.5	32.8	33.2	33.5	33.8	34.1	34.5	34.8	35.1
36	15.3	15.6	15.9	16.2	16.5	16.8	17.1	17.4	17.7	92	33.0	33.4	33.7	34.0	34.4	34.7	35.0	35.3	35.7
38	16.0	16.3	16.6	16.9	17.2	17.5	17.8	18.1	18.5	94	33.6	33.9	34.2	34.6	34.9	35.2	35.6	35.9	36.2
40	16.7	17.0	17.3	17.6	17.9	18.3	18.6	18.9	19.2	96	34.1	34.4	34.8	35.1	35.4	35.8	36.1	36.4	36.8
42	17.4	17.7	18.0	18.3	18.7	19.0	19.3	19.6	19.9	98	34.6	34.9	35.3	35.6	35.9	36.3	36.6	36.9	37.3
44	18.1	18.4	18.7	19.1	19.4	19.7	20.0	20.3	20.6	100	35.1	35.5	35.8	36.1	36.5	36.8	37.1	37.5	37.8
46	18.8	19.1	19.4	19.8	20.1	20.4	20.7	21.0	21.3	102	35.6	36.0	36.3	36.6	37.0	37.3	37.6	38.0	38.3
48	19.5	19.8	20.1	20.4	20.8	21.1	21.4	21.7	22.0	104	36.1	36.5	36.8	37.1	37.5	37.8	38.1	38.5	38.8
50	20.2	20.5	20.8	21.1	21.4	21.8	22.1	22.4	22.7	106	36.6	36.9	37.3	37.6	37.9	38.3	38.6	39.0	39.3
52	20.9	21.2	21.5	21.8	22.1	22.4	22.8	23.1	23.4	108	37.1	37.4	37.8	38.1	38.4	38.8	39.1	39.4	39.8
54	21.6	21.9	22.2	22.5	22.8	23.1	23.4	23.7	24.1	110	37.6	37.9	38.2	38.6	38.9	39.2	39.6	39.9	40.3
56	22.2	22.5	22.8	23.2	23.5	23.8	24.1	24.4	24.7	112	38.0	38.4	38.7	39.0	39.4	39.7	40.0	40.4	40.7
58	22.9	23.2	23.5	23.8	24.1	24.5	24.8	25.1	25.4	114	38.5	38.8	39.2	39.5	39.8	40.2	40.5	40.8	41.2
60	23.5	23.8	24.2	24.5	24.8	25.1	25.4	25.7	26.1	116	38.9	39.3	39.6	39.9	40.3	40.6	41.0	41.3	41.6
62	24.2	24.5	24.8	25.1	25.4	25.8	26.1	26.4	26.7	118	39.4	39.7	40.0	40.4	40.7	41.1	41.4	41.7	42.1
64	24.8	25.1	25.4	25.8	26.1	26.4	26.7	27.0	27.4	120	39.8	40.1	40.5	40.8	41.2	41.5	41.8	42.2	42.5
66	25.4	25.8	26.1	26.4	26.7	27.0	27.4	27.7	28.0	122	40.2	40.6	40.9	41.2	41.6	41.9	42.3	42.6	42.9
68	26.1	26.4	26.7	27.0	27.4	27.7	28.0	28.3	28.6	124	40.6	41.0	41.3	41.7	42.0	42.3	42.7	43.0	43.4
70	26.7	27.0	27.3	27.7	28.0	28.3	28.6	28.9	29.3	126	41.0	41.4	41.7	42.1	42.4	42.7	43.1	43.4	43.8

Example: If a women's age is 39 years and the sum of three skinfolds equals 58 mm, then her percent fat is 24.1%.

Table was calculated from A.S. Jackson, M.L. Pollock, and A. Ward. Generalized equations for predicting body density of women. *Medicine and Science in Sports and Exercise* 12:175-182, 1980.

Table D.2. *Male Percent Body Fat Conversion from the Sum of Three Skinfolds.*

Sum of 3 Skinfolds (mm)	18-22	23-27	28-32	33-37	38-42	43-47	48-52	53-57	58-62	Sum of 3 Skinfolds (mm)	18-22	23-27	28-32	33-37	38-42	43-47	48-52	53-57	58-62
10	1.6	2.2	2.7	3.2	3.8	4.3	4.8	5.4	5.9	64	18.0	18.5	19.1	19.7	20.3	20.8	21.4	22.0	22.6
12	2.3	2.8	3.4	3.9	4.4	5.0	5.5	6.1	6.6	66	18.5	19.1	19.7	20.2	20.8	21.4	22.0	22.6	23.1
14	2.9	3.5	4.0	4.6	5.1	5.6	6.2	6.7	7.3	68	19.1	19.6	20.2	20.8	21.4	21.9	22.5	23.1	23.7
16	3.6	4.1	4.7	5.2	5.7	6.3	6.8	7.4	7.9	70	19.6	20.2	20.8	21.3	21.9	22.5	23.1	23.7	24.2
18	4.2	4.8	5.3	5.9	6.4	6.9	7.5	8.0	8.6	72	20.1	20.7	21.3	21.9	22.5	23.0	23.6	24.2	24.8
20	4.9	5.4	6.0	6.5	7.0	7.6	8.1	8.7	9.2	74	20.7	21.2	21.8	22.4	23.0	23.6	24.2	24.7	25.3
22	5.5	6.1	6.6	7.1	7.7	8.2	8.8	9.3	9.9	76	21.2	21.8	22.4	22.9	23.5	24.1	24.7	25.3	25.9
24	6.1	6.7	7.2	7.8	8.3	8.9	9.4	10.0	10.5	78	21.7	22.3	22.9	23.5	24.0	24.6	25.2	25.8	26.4
26	6.8	7.3	7.9	8.4	9.0	9.5	10.1	10.6	11.2	80	22.2	22.8	23.4	24.0	24.6	25.2	25.7	26.3	26.9
28	7.4	7.9	8.5	9.0	9.6	10.1	10.7	11.2	11.8	82	22.7	23.3	23.9	24.5	25.1	25.7	26.3	26.8	27.4
30	8.0	8.6	9.1	9.7	10.2	10.8	11.3	11.9	12.4	84	23.3	23.8	24.4	25.0	25.6	26.2	26.8	27.4	28.0
32	8.6	9.2	9.7	10.3	10.8	11.4	11.9	12.5	13.1	86	23.8	24.3	24.9	25.5	26.1	26.7	27.3	27.9	28.5
34	9.2	9.8	10.3	10.9	11.5	12.0	12.6	13.1	13.7	88	24.3	24.8	25.4	26.0	26.6	27.2	27.8	28.4	29.0
36	9.9	10.4	11.0	11.5	12.1	12.6	13.2	13.7	14.3	90	24.7	25.3	25.9	26.5	27.1	27.7	28.3	28.9	29.5
38	10.5	11.0	11.6	12.1	12.7	13.2	13.8	14.4	14.9	92	25.2	25.8	26.4	27.0	27.6	28.2	28.8	29.4	30.0
40	11.1	11.6	12.2	12.7	13.3	13.8	14.4	15.0	15.5	94	25.7	26.3	26.9	27.5	28.1	28.7	29.3	29.9	30.5
42	11.7	12.2	12.8	13.3	13.9	14.5	15.0	15.6	16.1	96	26.2	26.8	27.4	28.0	28.6	29.2	29.8	30.4	31.0
44	12.3	12.8	13.4	13.9	14.5	15.1	15.6	16.2	16.7	98	26.7	27.3	27.9	28.4	29.0	29.6	30.2	30.8	31.4
46	12.9	13.4	14.0	14.5	15.1	15.7	16.2	16.8	17.3	100	27.1	27.7	28.3	28.9	29.5	30.1	30.7	31.3	31.9
48	13.4	14.0	14.6	15.1	15.7	16.2	16.8	17.4	17.9	102	27.6	28.2	28.8	29.4	30.0	30.6	31.2	31.8	32.4
50	14.0	14.6	15.1	15.7	16.3	16.8	17.4	18.0	18.5	104	28.1	28.7	29.3	29.9	30.5	31.1	31.7	32.3	32.9
52	14.6	15.2	15.7	16.3	16.9	17.4	18.0	18.6	19.1	106	28.5	29.1	29.7	30.3	30.9	31.5	32.1	32.7	33.3
54	15.2	15.7	16.3	16.9	17.4	18.0	18.6	19.1	19.7	108	29.0	29.6	30.2	30.8	31.4	32.0	32.6	33.2	33.8
56	15.7	16.3	16.9	17.4	18.0	18.6	19.1	19.7	20.3	110	29.4	30.0	30.6	31.2	31.8	32.4	33.0	33.6	34.2
58	16.3	16.9	17.4	18.0	18.6	19.1	19.7	20.3	20.9	112	29.8	30.4	31.0	31.6	32.3	32.9	33.5	34.1	34.7
60	16.9	17.4	18.0	18.6	19.1	19.7	20.3	20.9	21.4	114	30.3	30.9	31.5	32.1	32.7	33.3	33.9	34.5	35.1
62	17.4	18.0	18.6	19.1	19.7	20.3	20.9	21.4	22.0	116	30.7	31.3	31.9	32.5	33.1	33.7	34.3	34.9	35.6

Example: If a man's age is 45 years and the sum of three skinfolds equals 50 mm, then his percent fat is 16.8%.

Table was calculated from A.S. Jackson and M.L. Pollock. Generalized equations for predicting body density of men. *British Journal of Nutrition* 40:497-504, 1978.

Table D.3. *Estimates of Ideal Body Fat for Different Age Groups*

Age Group		Average % Fat	Ideal % Fat
18-24	male	12	10
	female	22	18
25-30	male	15	10
	female	25	18
31-40	male	17	12
	female	27	20
41-50	male	20	15
	female	30	23
51-60	male	24	17
	female	34	25
61-70	male	27	20
	female	37	28

Adapted with permission from T.R. Thomas and C.J. Zebas. *Scientific Exercise Training.* Copyright © 1984 by Kendall/Hunt Publishing Co.

Estimation of Percent Body Fat
Record Sheet

JACKSON AND POLLOCK TECHNIQUE

Name _____ Sex _____ Date _____

Age _____ (yrs)

Weight _____(kg) _____(lbs)

(Measurements on Dominant Side)

Skinfolds: Women

  1. Triceps_____ mm

  2. Suprailium _____ mm

  3. Thigh_____ mm

  4. Sum of skinfolds_____ mm

Skinfolds: Men

  1. Chest _____ mm

  2. Abdominal_____ mm

  3. Thigh _____ mm

  4. Sum of skinfolds_____ mm

Convert sum of the skinfolds to % fat using Table D.1 or D.2.

PERCENT FAT _____

% Fat Changes

Evaluation Date	% Fat	Body Weight
1st test _____	_____	_____
2nd test _____	_____	_____
3rd test _____	_____	_____